TWAYNE'S WORLD AUTHORS SERIES

A Survey of the World's Literature

Sylvia E. Bowman, Indiana University

GENERAL EDITOR

POLAND

Dr. Irene Nagurski

EDITOR

Jan Kochanowski

TWAS 330

Jan Kochanowski

Jan Kochanowski

By DAVID WELSH

University of Michigan

Twayne Publishers, Inc.   ::   New York

Library of Congress Cataloging in Publication Data

Welsh, David J
    Jan Kochanowski.

    (Twayne's world authors series, TWAS 330. Poland)
    Bibliography: p. 151.
    1. Kochanowski, Jan, 1530–1584.
PG7157.K6Z92   891.8'5'13 [B]   74-6391
ISBN 0–8057–2490–7

102173

FEB 18 '75

To Elizabeth

Contents

About the Author

David Welsh has published several novels, critical studies in Polish and Russian literature, essays and book reviews as well as a number of translations from the Polish. For these activities Professor Welsh has received awards from the American Council of Polish Cultural clubs and the Writers' and Artists' Union (Warsaw). His translation of *The Doll* (Lalka) by Bolesław Prus (Twayne, 1972) was nominated for a National Book award.

Professor Welsh became interested in Polish language and literature when holding an appointment at the British embassy in Warsaw, and has visited Poland a number of times. Since coming to the United States in 1961, he has taught Polish and Russian languages and literatures at the University of Michigan, Ann Arbor.

Preface

Jan Kochanowski (1530–1584) created Polish poetry for his own age and for all later generations of Polish poets. Poets before him had written in the vernacular, but they all lacked the one power which Kochanowski possessed—that of transforming his native language into an instrument for the creation of poetry rather than verse (no matter what other admirable qualities that verse may possess).

In Poland, dozens of editions of Kochanowski's poetry have been printed and reprinted, in collected or individual editions, ever since his death, which testifies to his consistently elevated place in Polish literature. Hundreds of books and scholarly essays accompany the works themselves. Almost no other European poet of Kochanowski's generation has remained alive to his fellow-countrymen in this way. Echoes of his poetry resound throughout Polish literature and life, through the seventeenth century to Ignacy Krasicki, Adam Mickiewicz, Cyprian Norwid, and into our own time. His presence is always there, and Polish literature cannot be appreciated without an understanding of this presence.

Genius is not to be explained, still less explicated. The present study, therefore, attempts merely to describe some aspects of Kochanowski's art, setting it in a Polish and also a European context. In addition to being prolific, as most major writers are, Kochanowski displayed remarkable variety in his work, as this study shows. He wrote much in Latin, including elegies and odes. In Polish he composed political, satirical, and narrative poems; epigrams, much lyrical poetry (songs), and threnodies (laments); a poetic drama; and a complete translation of the Old Testament Psalms. His prose works included a treatise on Polish orthography, a dialogue between a gentleman and a priest, a series of apothegms, and other minor works. Unfortunately only two personal letters have survived, so that our knowledge of Kochanowski as an individual must be drawn almost entirely from his work and occasional references to him by his contemporaries.

Acknowledgments and thanks for encouragement, advice, and assistance are due to Ms. Elizabeth Bardswell, Professor A. M. Kleimola, Mr. K. Peczkowski and the Authors' Agency (Warsaw). Opportunity to write the study was provided by the American Council of Learned Societies, the Rackham Graduate School at the University of Michigan, and the Center for Russian and East European Studies, Ann Arbor.

The translations on pp. 47–48, and 87 (The "Song" and "In Defence of Drunkards") are reprinted from *Five Centuries of Polish Poetry 1450–1970* (Second edition) translated by Jerzy Peterkiewicz and Burns Singer, with new poems translated in collaboration with Jon Stallworthy. Reprinted by permission of Oxford University Press.

Unless otherwise stated, other translations are mine.

DAVID WELSH

University of Michigan

Chronology

1530   Jan Kochanowski born in Sycyna (Central Poland), in a moderately well-to-do family of Polish gentry.

1544–   Study at the Cracow Academy, later to be the Jagellonian
1549   University.

1551–   Kochanowski in attendance at the court of Prince Albrecht
1552   of Prussia, Königsberg.

1552–   Three journeys to Italy, with studies at the University of
1559   Padua, and a brief visit to France.

1560   Kochanowski's Court period, in attendance on King Zygmunt
1568   August, in Cracow and elsewhere. In this period were printed *A Game of Chess* (1562), *Susanna* (1562), *Concord* (1564), and *The Satyr* (1564).

1570   Kochanowski retires to a small country estate at Czarnolas, inherited from his father, and his most productive period as a poet begins.

1570–   Kochanowski translates the Psalms into Polish.
1578

1578   His rhetorical tragedy *Dismissal of the Grecian Envoys* commissioned and performed near Warsaw.

1580   A cycle of *Laments* composed on the death of a daughter.

1584   Death of Jan Kochanowski. His collected *Epigrams* first printed.

1586   Kochanowski's collection of *Songs* printed for the first time, posthumously.

CHAPTER 1

Poland's Renaissance

THE Renaissance reached Poland somewhat late—as it did England. Although cultural movements cannot be dated precisely, the year 1518 may be taken as an approximate beginning for the Polish Age of Gold. This was the year when the elegant Italian princess Bona Sforza married King Zygmunt I (Sigismund) and came to the royal court in Cracow with attendant Italian noblemen, musicians, artists, architects, and even landscape gardeners. To be sure, King Zygmunt already had close ties with almost all the countries of Western Europe, forged at the Congress of Vienna in 1515, and he did much to promote humanistic culture at his court. But Italian influences were strongest.

Zygmunt I had been elected King of Poland and Grand Duke of Lithuania in 1506, at the age of forty. The last king of the Jagellonian dynasty, he was educated by Italian teachers (his mother had been Italian), and as a refined humanist, he was much influenced by Western standards. Described as "wise and provident, pious and just, loyal in politics and attached to peace,"[1] he promised to make a great ruler of Poland. But he proved to be lacking in energy and was faced with numerous problems throughout his long reign (to 1548): these were political and territorial (wars with Muscovy), also religious (the Reformation, which flowed in a "broad though shallow current" across Poland).[2] Social unrest was rife also; the gentry, who constituted the most powerful class in Poland for many years, had acquired rights in the mid-1400's, and consolidated them fifty years later. But King Zygmunt had no confidence in their loyalty, and relied on certain families he himself had elevated to the aristocracy. Disappointed, the gentry placed their hopes in his son and successor King Zygmunt August.

13

The latter, however, only widened the gap between the throne and gentry; his reign was marked by internal unrest, as well as continuing hostilities with Muscovy and Sweden. The question of union with Lithuania plagued Poland for the first decade of Zygmunt August's reign, and was finally resolved in 1569, with the Union of Lublin—an event with effects as far-reaching as the Act of Union between England and Scotland (1603). The events and situation in Poland all find a place in Kochanowski's poetry.

I *The Life*

Kochanowski as an individual is as little known as Shakespeare. Only two likenesses survive: a woodcut (1578) of a gentleman with mustaches and penetrating eyes, wearing a costume of the court of King Zygmunt I; and a bust on his tomb, with a melancholy look, wearing a beard and holding what seems to be a pair of gloves, or roll of papers. A few surviving letters add little to our knowledge of his life.

He belonged to a family of gentry; his father made a considerable fortune, and his mother was also of a wealthy family. His younger brothers Mikołaj and Andrzej made contributions to Polish literature; the former translated Plutarch into Polish, the latter the *Aeneid* of Virgil. A nephew, Piotr, translated Tasso's *Jerusalem Delivered* in 1618. This epic work has rightly been acclaimed as one of the national classics of Polish poetry, and opened new perspectives during the Baroque period (seventeenth century).[3]

Kochanowski enrolled in the Cracow Academy in 1544. His name appears on the list of students for that year. But there is no record of what he studied, or how long he attended. Outbreaks of plague in the same year, and the death of his father in 1547, obliged him to return home. He never graduated.

At this time, the Academy was a hotbed of Protestant and Calvinistic doctrines, which spread into Poland from Luther's Germany. Although there is little evidence, we may suppose that Kochanowski was subjected to these influences. He may have proceeded from Cracow to Wrocław (formerly Breslau) *en route* for the University of Wittenberg, that "mecca of

Protestants" in the sixteenth century. He was in Poland again in January, 1550, to settle family matters connected with an inheritance. Two years later, Prince Albrecht of Königsberg (East Prussia)—a center of Lutheranism—provided Kochanowski with funds to pursue his education in Italy; he visited Rome and Naples, then returned to Königsberg from May 1555 to April 1556. Prince Albrecht provided Kochanowski with more funds to enable him to revisit Italy, and this time he attended the University of Padua for some time. Literary scholars have investigated Kochanowski's Italian journeys, but to little purpose. Did he visit Rome or Venice? Or Petrarch's tomb, near Padua? Or even the Sabine farm of Horace? We shall never know, and in any case the speculations are futile.

His mother's death took him back to Poland until September, 1557, after which his longest and last visit to Italy took place between Autumn, 1557, and the late Spring of 1559. Then he returned to Poland via France, where he may have met or at least seen the Pléiade poet Ronsard. Thus Kochanowski spent some three years altogether in Italy, at intervals, during the most formative years of his life, the twenties.

In Poland, Kochanowski obtained appointments of various kinds at the royal court, and at the courts of Bishop Padniewski (Cracow) and the Palatine Firlej (Lublin), acting as "secretary and courtier." During this period he composed most of his "political poetry" and panegyrics on various occasions, often commissioned by and addressed to noblemen on whose patronage he was largely reliant. But from what little we know of him, Kochanowski was not suited to court life, and at the end of 1570 he retired to a small country estate known as Czarnolas, where he married and enjoyed his most creative period until his death in 1584. He composed all his major works at Czarnolas.

II *Kochanowski's Contemporaries*

The first Polish writer to use his own name was Mikołaj Rej (1505–1569); earlier writers were generally known by their first names, differentiating themselves by adding their place of birth or habitation (Biernat of Lublin), or a Latin name. Rej has been called "the father of Polish literature" and "the Polish

Dante," not as a poet, but because he fathered the national literature as Dante had fathered Italian poetry.[4] Rej wrote exclusively in Polish and admitted he was no scholar, having no Latin or Greek. But both the above quotations are open to question: Rej was a Protestant, consequently his works were regarded after his death as heretical and fell into obscurity for some three centuries.

Rej's ignorance of the classical authors betrays itself in his work, which is exceedingly copious both in verse and prose. As we know, most major writers are copious, but Rej's verse displays traces of hasty, even careless writing, characterized, for instance, by the composition of couplets in which the second line is put in for the sake of the rhyme, rather than the sense. To be sure, this was a common enough fault of most medieval writers, and the epithet "medieval" is apt for Rej's verse (his prose is more interesting stylistically).

All his writings without exception were meant to teach; like the secular versifiers of the fifteenth century, with their poems on how to behave at table, and so on, Rej clearly thought that the function of literature was to teach, or persuade people how to be virtuous. But he also saw that teaching must be entertaining. He attained this entertainment value through his vocabulary, which is remarkably rich and colloquial, using words drawn from a wide lexical range—terms of hunting, fishing, farming, foods and drinks, articles of dress, household goods. Many are now archaic and have even been forgotten. He made use also of Polish proverbs and folk sayings, preserving them for later generations.

Rej's attitude toward his own work was also medieval in that he never hesitated to borrow anything from other writers that suited his purpose. The concept of plagiarism does not come into literature until considerably later.

The other Polish poet of the sixteenth century whose work continues to be read is Mikołaj Sęp-Szarzyński (1530–1581), in many ways a complete contrast to both Rej and Kochanowski. He left only a handful of sonnets, lyrics and Latin poetry, not printed until 1601. As Rej looked back to the Middle Ages and Kochanowski represented Renaissance humanism at its peak, so Sęp-Szarzyński's work looks forward to the Baroque poetry of the seventeenth century. Preoccupied by feelings of his own sinfulness and unworthiness (he was a convert from Protestantism to Catholicism at the age of eighteen), Sęp-Szarzyński's sonnets resound with the anguished tones that echo throughout Polish poetry of the Baroque period. Admittedly, he looks back to some degree to the mysticism of the Middle Ages, which is totally foreign to Kochanowski, whose view of the well-ordered harmonious world of the humanists only falters toward the end of his life in the *Treny* (Laments), written on the death of a small daughter.

Already in Sęp-Szarzyński's sonnets we see the flowing and regular metrical patterns established by Kochanowski on the verge of breaking down. Here the movement is stronger, more powerful, sometimes almost dislocated under the weight of the spiritual conflicts the poet seeks to express. Indeed, the sonnets may well be described as intricate metaphysical arguments expressed in highly condensed language. Kochanowski's preference for simplicity, clarity, and order in his poetry gives way to Sęp-Szarzyński's intricacy, complexity, and tension—characteristic features of the Baroque in all the arts. Certainly, attempts have been made to find Baroque elements in Kochanowski's last period, especially the *Laments,* but Professor Janusz Pelc has successfully refuted them.[5]

Other interesting poets abounded in sixteenth-century Poland, each with his own individual poetic voice. Most were younger than Kochanowski, and almost all express their debt to him in various ways: Simon Simonides (1558–1629), who preferred the Latinized version of his Polish name Szymon Szymonowicz and who is remembered for his *Sielanki* (Idylls) of 1614, with many delightful classical echoes in a Polish setting; Sebastian Klonowic (1545–1602), who began writing (like Simonides) in Latin, then published a long allegorical poem comparing the life of man to a journey by river (*Flis,* The Boatman)[6] and other works betraying a medieval turn of mind, with some touches of realism. Nor does this section take into account the minor writers of verse and prose who flourished, as writers flourished in Elizabethan England and elsewhere in Western Europe.

III   On the Revolutions of the Heavenly Bodies

The year 1543 had marked a turning point in European scientific thought, only comparable to the later discoveries of Galileo and Kepler, and—in our own time—those of Einstein. In that year, the astronomer Copernicus (who was Polish although he wrote in Latin, the international language of science) published his treatise *On the Revolutions of the Heavenly Bodies,* in which he effectively altered the entire medieval world-picture. Here he demonstrated scientifically that our world is not the center of the universe, nor was it created exclusively for man's benefit. His findings did not, of course, become common knowledge for many years, but the main ideas penetrated into man's awareness, despite attacks by both Catholic and Protestant churches.[7] Men began to doubt the evidence of their senses: if mankind and our world were not gradually working their way toward perfection (as the Middle Ages believed), might they not be working toward decay? The theme of the world's decay appears in European literature at this period with increasing frequency.

IV   *Christian Latin Poetry*

Kochanowski's earliest poetry to be printed was composed in Latin. Many poets in Poland, as elsewhere in Europe, cultivated Latin as a medium for their art. The vernacular was adequate for "private" poetry intended for friends and circulated for the most part in manuscript copies. But "public" poetry celebrating important events—the birth of princes or the death of kings—intended to immortalize eminent persons, could most appropriately be written in Latin. They believed that "poets who lasting marble seek / Must carve in Latin, or in Greek" (Edmund Waller). Kochanowski's near contemporaries Sęp-Szarzyński, Klonowic, Simonides and Maciej Sarbiewski all wrote in Latin as fluently as in Polish; indeed, the last-named used Latin exclusively, and was famed all over Europe for his poetry. The University of Torun fostered a school of neo-Latin poets, which flourished until the 1760's.[8] This method of proceeding was by no means confined to Poland, of course; in England, John Milton (among others) wrote Latin verses as well as he did

English. Before the "Nativity Ode," he wrote more poetry in
Latin than in English, and Dr. Leavis holds that the best of
Milton's Latin poetry is "at least as good as the best of the
English."[9]

In the sixteenth century, after all, most of the vernacular
languages were still at a comparatively early stage of development, and poets felt their own languages to be inadequate as a
means of expression. The task of poets was to remedy this. All
the same, the finest poetry they knew was in Latin—Horace,
Virgil, Ovid, and the other classical authors of antiquity. Their
education consisted almost entirely of studying the classical
authors; and, when they turned to writing in their own languages, naturally poets took the classics as models.

But the classical authors were, of course, "pagan" writers.
With the passing of time, specifically Christian poets began
writing (from about the fourth century A.D.), and there exists
today a corpus of this poetry, largely unexplored.[10] For the
most part, this is the poetry of rhetoric, designed primarily to
surprise and delight by reason of its ingenuity; there are poems
shaped in the form of a cross or star, poems that can be read
backwards as well as forwards, acrostics in which the first letter
of each line spells out a name. A great many of the poems are
hymns or didactic in purpose. Though such displays of wit
can hardly be accounted "poetry," versifying of this kind had its
uses; by confronting writers with purely technical problems
of form or "shape," such verses served as exercises in skill.

Of more importance, however, was the change that the Latin
language itself underwent over the ten centuries between the
death of Horace in Imperial Rome and the advent of Christianity
in Poland (965 A.D.). Classical Latin poetry was always patterned on the quantity of vowels (long or short according to
set rules of position): every line in a poem was composed
according to a pattern of feet, made up of arrangements of
syllables (long/short/short, for instance), the number of feet
to a line also being fixed.[11] This manner of writing poetry sounds
restrictive, even rigid, and the writers of Christian Latin poetry
gradually abandoned it, though we do not know why. Perhaps
they forgot the rules. Certainly, their pronunciation of Latin
must have varied considerably from that of the ancients them-

selves. In any case, later writers began patterning their lines on the number of syllables in each line, ignoring the rules of quantity. They also introduced the use of rhymes to bind together the otherwise loose syllabic lines.[12] Classical Latin poets rarely, if ever, used rhyme.

Both these developments later affected Polish poetry in the vernacular. When poets trained in the writing of Christian Latin poetry turned to their own language, they modeled vernacular poems on the syllabic, rhymed poetry with which they were already familiar. Consequently, Polish poetry (like French) has always been patterned by the number of syllables to a line.

Kochanowski composed some seven thousand lines of Latin poetry, a third of his total output. He never attempted an epic, but practiced other prestigious genres, such as the ode, elegy, and epigram. His Latin poetry may be dismissed as passive transplantation of an alien literary culture to Polish soil, and indeed, the question arises whether his Latin poetry (now unread save by the few, or in translation) can properly be considered along with his Polish poetry. But the distinction would not have troubled Kochanowski himself; and no study of his art can ignore these works.

V Odes and Elegies

The ode as a genre was highly regarded in classical antiquity, and continued to be so until the nineteenth century. The genre flourished during the period of Romanticism (Keats, Shelley, Schiller, Mickiewicz all composed one or more odes). Traditionally, an ode is a poem addressed to a person, object, or abstraction: Youth, Freedom, a Grecian vase, the West Wind, Peter the Great—all have been apostrophized in odes. In a sense, we are permitted to overhear the poet speaking, in tones which may range from the sublime to the ironical. Thus, an ode cannot exist without an audience, and this may be one reason for its frequency in Latin. Roman poets seem to have been reticent about expressing their personal feelings in poetry. So they liked to have a reason or excuse for writing. The odes of Horace, the most admired examples of the genre, are either addressed to other people or celebrate special occasions (e.g., the Cleopatra ode, I, 37, written on news of her death).

Kochanowski's "little book of odes," as he called it, conforms to the classical pattern. In some he addresses individuals such as Henri de Valois, who was king of Poland for six months in 1574, until he took a dislike to the place, and fled; or wealthy magnates, discussing their policies and supporting this, that, or the other faction in contemporary political life. Some odes are addressed to mythological beings, or personified abstracts (Concord); yet others are occasional, in the proper meaning of that term, being written to celebrate an occasion, such as King Stefan Batory's recapture of the town of Polock from Ivan the Terrible in 1579.

VI *Elegies*

The revival of classical poetic forms by Renaissance poets resulted in some uncertainty regarding nomenclature. An example was the use of the word "elegy" to designate poems widely differing in length, form, and content. The principal classical inspiration appears to have come, not from the Latin elegiac poets, but from the laments of Ovid's lover in his *Heroides*. The prestige of the elegy was, in any case, high, and poets continued writing elegies until the eighteenth century, the best known in English being Thomas Gray's "Elegy Written in a Country Churchyard" (1750).

In Latin poetry, the elegy was identifiable by its meter, an alternating sequence of dactylic (long/short/short syllables) hexameters and pentameters, a meter occasionally used by English poets as a feat of ingenuity: "In the hexameter rises the fountain's silvery column / In the pentameter falling in melody back" (Tennyson) or Longfellow's "So the hexameter rising and singing with cadence sonorous / Falls, and in refluent rhythm back the pentameter flows." Originally, the elegy was a song of lamentation for the dead, but with time it became the form of poetry most suited to a reflective mind. Indeed, Coleridge said of the elegy that it "may treat of any subject . . . but always and exclusively with reference to the poet himself. As he will feel regret for the past or desire for the future, so sorrow and love become the principal themes of elegy" (*Table Talk*, October 23, 1833).

Kochanowski's Latin elegies look back to the Italian poet Petrarch rather than to Ovid.[13] Petrarch's *Canzoniere* (1380) served as a model for innumerable love-sick poets throughout the Renaissance, who complained in verse that their love is "unhappy" and their mistresses "cruel." Kochanowski's "Lidia" is as cruel as any of these conventional ladies, though he claims there is "nothing he would not do for her sake" (II, 5). Lidia is "accursed," yet Kochanowski continues to celebrate her beauty in "smooth rhymes" (II, 6). His love is Petrarchan in being restless, suffering, and consuming, and he expresses his unhappy lot with sighs and tears. Unlike Petrarch, however, Kochanowski does not dwell on the physical charms of his lady, nor does he enfold her in the spirituality so characteristic of Petrarch's Laura.

Kochanowski's Lidia has been identified.[14] But this identification is of little help in approaching the poetry. We can never say, in poetry of this kind, whether the poem is based on personal experience, or whether it is the result of reading other people's poetry of a similar kind. After all, personal experience *and* the experience of reading other poets are both valid sources for creativity; nor is a poem better, or worse, for being known to derive from one or the other experience. Much poetry originates from both sources simultaneously. Nor can we dismiss a poem because its situation has been used successfully before. The critical question is whether the poet has added something of his own to a convention.

VII *The Grecian Garland*

The Latin poetry of classical antiquity was not Kochanowski's only source of inspiration. Greek poetry also provided him with models to imitate.[15] The study of Greek language and literature, although never entirely obsolete in Western Europe, was overshadowed by study of the Latin writers, but Greek was taught by professors at the Cracow Academy in the 1530's, and Greek authors were being printed there also. Kochanowski acquired sufficient Greek to translate passages from Homer and Euripides into Polish, some two hundred years before the great eighteenth-century translations were made. Kochanowski's interest in these two Greek authors is remarkable in view of the marked lack of enthusiasm for them among Renaissance theoreticians of poetry, who preferred the decorum of Virgil's *Aeneid* to the less polished *Iliad*.

But Kochanowski's study of Greek had little practical value in the development of his art. He never attempted the epic strain, and his one play (discussed in chapter 5) owes nothing to the Greeks, being a characteristic rhetorical tragedy of the sixteenth century. However, knowledge of Greek opened for him a treasury of Greek poetry in the *Greek Anthology*. This vast collection of over four thousand poems was collected over sixteen centuries, from Euripides and Plato to the Italian Renaissance. First printed in 1474, the *Anthology* was avidly read and imitated by poets in England, France, Italy, and Poland—among others. It has retained its vitality to the present, as witness a contemporary rendering (London, 1973), though many of the verses contained in the *Anthology* are trivial and uninspired.[16]

All the poems in the *Anthology* are "epigrams"—another word that has changed its meaning since the ancient Greeks used it to denote anything written on a surface; magic spells engraved on wood or pieces of bone were "epigrams," as were inscriptions on tombs. In the fourth century B.C., Greeks conceived the notion that inscriptions on tombs should be poetic, and poets were commissioned to compose them. Many of the epigrams in the *Anthology* are of this kind, though we should call them "epitaphs." Nor were Greek epigrams witty; what mattered was that the epigram be appropriate to the occasion for which it was written—simple, elegant, and usually reticent in tone.

Sixteenth-century poets had their own ways of utilizing the enormous store of verses in the *Anthology*. Some made straightforward translations, others produced "multiple translations" of the same poem; a forgotten English poet John Stockwell composed four hundred and fifty different versions of one epigram. Other poets wrote "replies" to a Greek epigram. Yet another technique was "imitation," a process somewhat different from translation.

Translation and imitation were of considerable interest to Renaissance writers, in Poland as elsewhere.[17] Both arts were primarily regarded as having a patriotic function of enriching the vernacular languages, as was the case in Poland when Łukasz Górnicki produced his version of Castiglione's *Il Cortegiano* (1528). To make his point, Górnicki entitled his version *Dworzanin polski* (The Polish Courtier) when the work was printed in 1566. He transposed the setting from Urbino to near Cracow, introduced Polish characters and Polish anecdotes, and removed the women characters entirely.[18] Even so, the Italian original had many words and phrases for which the Polish language possessed no equivalents at that time, particularly in fields such as philosophy, music, the fine arts, and literature. In a sense, Górnicki did for Polish prose what Kochanowski was doing for poetry. When Sir Thomas Hoby made his English translation of *Il Cortegiano* in 1561, he experienced precisely the same difficulties Górnicki was to have with Polish five years later, and he solved them in the same way—transposing, adding, omitting.

Imitation was also a source for enriching a poet's vocabulary and technique; by sedulously imitating, a poet could render the excellencies of the original in his own language, and when imitations were made of epigrams in the *Anthology*, it was proper to entitle them "From the Greek."

Though Kochanowski's epigrams are in Latin (he also composed many in Polish, but these are not considered until chapter 6), they are also close in spirit to the Greek. He announces his preference for short poems in the first of the epigrams, which is addressed to the reader. His topics, he says, range from the pleasures of life, with wit and satire, sometimes reflecting on morality, love, and death, interspersed with droll anecdotes and some obscenity. He uses the epigram to complain yet again of his cruel mistress, and indeed states that he envies Petrarch, who, on dying, crossed the river of forgetfulness to be united with the beautiful Laura.

He celebrates the pleasures of companionship and wine as Horace had done fifteen hundred years before: "My dear friends, / While Fate is favorable, / Let each man drink up / His goblet to the dregs." The pagan gods and goddesses of mythology are invoked: Kochanowski calls upon Venus to return to him his "youthful looks, / Or favor an old man as you did when he was young." He praises Bacchus, "the father of dancing and the friend of song . . . Comrade of Cupid, and favorite of Venus." These three personages help us "enjoy life while we can," and Kochanowski reminds us that "no one can guess the future, / Or man's uncertain fate." Here already we have a statement of one of the major themes which recur throughout Kochanowski's poetry, especially in his Polish *Songs* and the *Laments*. After all, life in the sixteenth century was even more uncertain than life in our own times, and Kochanowski during his period at various courts knew full well that royal favor might at any time be withdrawn; and always, in the background, was the threat of wars, outbreaks of plague, religious intolerance.

Epitaphs commemorating dead persons also find a place in the collection. Indeed, the first of Kochanowski's poems to be printed was a Latin epitaph addressed to a certain Erasmus Kretkowski, who died in Padua in 1558. The epitaph appeared in a book printed in that city in 1560. Kochanowski respectfully lists Kretkowski's virtues, and describes his services to Poland as an envoy of King Zygmunt.[19]

Even in the mildly obscene epigrams, Kochanowski was following the *Greek Anthology*, which contains "scores of poems . . . quite unfit ever to have been written, edited, printed, or read."[20] This being the case, those of Kochanowski may remain in the obscurity of a foreign language. Their formal virtuosity makes some amends for the impropriety of their content.

CHAPTER 2

Cracow, Padua, Paris

THE difficulties of travel in the sixteenth century did not deter stouthearted men from making extensive journeys, sometimes for diplomatic or trading purposes, but more often to further their education. Chaucer visited Italy as early as 1372; Sir Philip Sidney was there in the mid-sixteenth century, and he visited Poland in the 1570's. Throughout the Renaissance, Italy was the destination of most travelers in Western Europe, just as Greece in the time of Horace had been the destination of young Romans. Generally, Poles preferred to visit Italy when they went abroad—a practice that continued well into the eighteenth century, when the young Ignacy Krasicki visited Rome in 1761. Though Germany was geographically closer, that country was a hotbed of heresy, as Lutheran and Calvinist dogma spread during the Reformation. To be sure, some Poles went there: Mikołaj Sęp-Szarzyński, the precursor of Baroque poetry in Polish, attended the University of Wittenberg; but later he went to Rome and was converted.

When the young Kochanowski enrolled at the University of Cracow (also called the Cracow Academy), in the summer of 1544, the university was already a center of the Reformation in Poland, and perhaps he was exposed to Lutheran doctrines which, among other things, deny the hierarchy of Christ, the Virgin Mary, and the saints, and leave man alone with God, no longer having the saints to intercede for him. Kochanowski never refers to the Virgin Mary or the saints, and even wrote an anti-papal elegy. But the Papacy was under attack from many quarters in the sixteenth century, as witness the celebrated "Epitaph to Rome" by the Italian humanist Vitalis, which was translated into English, French, and Polish by Edmund Spenser, Joachim du Bellay, and Mikołaj Sęp-Szarzyński, respectively.

26

I *Italy and Poetry*

Renaissance Italy was attractive to poets. The Italians were the first in Europe to make their own vernacular into a flexible instrument for poetry and prose. By the 1550's, Ronsard and the other Pléiade poets in France, conscious of the inadequacy of their own language, were beginning to achieve what the Italians had already done. The Poles and the English were still experimenting, trying to make their respective languages a suitable medium for poetry.

Italian poetry thus became both a model and a standard against which the vernaculars could be measured. Poetry was by no means the only field in which this realization was made. The Poles under King Zygmunt, like the English under Queen Elizabeth I, were ambitious patriots, eager to win a place for their countries alongside the greatest in Europe. In both countries, men went about this task with practical thoroughness, planning and ordering their campaigns as Sir Francis Drake planned his campaigns against the Spaniards. Poetry could be learned by practice, as the Latin authors demonstrated. Genius helped; but a sound knowledge of craftsmanship was as important. Kochanowski bequeathed this legacy to Polish literature, more markedly in the eighteenth century (as will be shown later).[1]

Of all the Italian poets, Petrarch (died 1374) was generally accorded the highest place, though Dante was respected. The latter, however, was inimitable while Petrarch's lyrics fulfilled all the requirements of sixteenth-century poetics; his stylistic refinement, elegance, devotion to classical antiquity— these gave him the rank of the father of Italian humanism at its finest. Then too, Petrarch had regarded the writing of poetry as an aristocratic craft, marked by conscious artistry. He was no revealer of Self, nor a critic of life; rather, he was a maker of beautiful things, with the emphasis on form more than on content; and that was always a feature of classical art, as compared to Baroque or Romantic art, where the emphasis is usually reversed. What Petrarch said was less interesting than the way he said it.

Kochanowski's interest in Italian poetry must, therefore, have been largely of a formal nature. Again his English contemporaries come to mind, for he was (like them) mainly attracted by the metrical virtuosity of Petrarch and his countless imitators. Kochanowski's predecessors in the writing of poetry in Polish had been deficient in precisely this respect.

The parallels between Kochanowski and his English contemporaries may be extended: in both countries, a sudden sense of discovery of their respective languages occurred. Shakespeare, Marlowe, and many other poets now began using the English language as though it were something new, a whole vast range of linguistic resources hitherto almost untapped. Kochanowski felt this of Polish; indeed, he claimed that he had been the first to set foot as a Pole on Caliope's heights (the goddess being the muse of heroic poetry).

The literary theory of the Polish Renaissance is not documented. Kochanowski left no account of his views on poetics such as Sir Philip Sidney's *Apologie for Poetrie* (1580), a treatise on method, principles, and prosody. All we can do is infer his views from his work. Whether he himself would have agreed with them is another matter. But he was certainly familiar with the numerous problems of writing in a vernacular language in the sixteenth century. His poetry is evidence that he successfully solved them.

II *Padua*

There were also nonliterary reasons for Poles to choose Italy as their destination when traveling abroad. Poland's ties with Italy had been firm since 1518, and Italian cultural and literary influences remained strong well into the seventeenth century, when Piotr Kochanowski (a distant relative) translated into Polish Torquato Tasso's epic poem *Jerusalem Delivered* in 1618, a work which transformed Polish poetry and established the Baroque style.[3]

Jan Kochanowski chose to study at the University of Padua, which was still a partly medieval town some thirty miles from Venice. In Kochanowski's day, however, the Gothic and Byzantine architecture of Padua was being radically changed by the erection of new buildings. Padua also had Roman remains.

The university was renowned throughout Europe as one of

the four great "fortresses of intellect," the others being Oxford, Paris, and Bologna. But the University of Padua was especially celebrated as a center of revolutionary scholarship, breaking away from medieval methods of study in the natural sciences, medicine, and philosophy. The faculty, many internationally famous, had vigorously started the secularization of study, separating experiment and observation from speculation or textual exegesis. The intellectual atmosphere prevailing at the university was brimming with new ideas; in this respect, it differed considerably from the declining Cracow Academy.[4]

The University of Padua was also a center for the Reformation movement, which was propagated there by visitors from England, Germany, and Switzerland.

Precisely what Kochanowski studied at Padua is not known; probably one of his masters was the eminent professor of rhetoric, Francesco Robortello (died 1567). If so, Kochanowski would have concentrated under Robortello on the study of classical texts from a philological rather than literary aspect. Robortello's commentary on Aristotle's *Poetics*, his best-known work, a copy of which Kochanowski owned, has retained sufficient critical importance to warrant its reprinting (Munich, 1969). His theory of textual criticism was influential during the Renaissance, and led to the rejection of earlier scholastic commentaries on Aristotle by concentrating on what Aristotle himself had written.

Another likely "master" of Kochanowski at Padua was the philosopher Tomitano, who occupied the chair of logic. He prided himself on being a free-thinker and declared that "just as there are many schools of philosophy, so one religion cannot exist by itself." He attacked the bigotry of certain colleagues, which drew the attention of the Inquisition to him as early as 1548. But Tomitano was able for a time to ward off these attacks, until 1555 when the Inquisition instituted proceedings against him; he was charged, among other crimes, of collaborating in the publication of one of the works of Erasmus of Amsterdam, which had been placed on the Index of Prohibited Books. But he repented his sins, and was later absolved. Nevertheless, this incident was one of the first attempts made by the Inquisition to restrict freedom of thought, leading to a number of notorious cases over the next two centuries.

Kochanowski undoubtedly studied logic at the Cracow Academy; all "freshmen" were obliged to do so. But the teaching methods at Cracow were still medieval, and logic was one of the most detested subjects on the syllabus. Indeed, the teaching of logic there was brought to a halt in 1554 by a student demonstration. However, Tomitano's method was "modern" and therefore popular. He was also a poet, known for sonnets and eclogues which were widely admired. His book on the use of the Italian language (1545) formed yet another contribution to the long-lasting debate on the use of vernacular languages as a medium for poetry. Tomitano believed that the Italian language was equal to the classical languages of antiquity and was suited to poetry. He even admitted colloquial language. But we cannot estimate how much Kochanowski was influenced by Tomitano's theories; all the same, the Italian may have encouraged Kochanowski in his vocation as poet; and he admired Petrarch.

Be this as it may, both Robortello and Tomitano were influential figures in sixteenth-century Italy, and Kochanowski's contacts with them—even if only at second-hand—brought him into the mainstream of European culture at its finest when he was still in his twenties.

As Kochanowski was not studying for a degree, he could choose any subjects that interested him. In addition to classical philology, logic, and rhetoric—which he might have studied at any university—he was no doubt drawn by the original, bold ideas being discussed in the philosophy department of the university, which was something of an intellectual phenomenon in the field. But we do not need to know precisely how Kochanowski spent his years in Italy; after all, he was by vocation a poet, not a philosopher, nor a theologian, nor a rhetorician— though philosophy, theology, and rhetoric all entered into his humanistic outlook. Indeed, the part which the university played in Kochanowski's development was that his stay there made him a humanist. Like many of his educated contemporaries, Kochanowski acquired from his university years not only a thorough knowledge of and love for the Greek and Latin authors, but his sojourn in Italy made him an individual with a cult for the beauty of this world combined with optimism and rationalism. He was never much interested in such matters as theology or the "after life" or the salvation of his or anybody's soul. This is one of the reasons why the poetry of Kochanowski was so highly regarded during Poland's Age of Enlightenment (1764–1796), when writers adopted much the same attitude as Kochanowski had done.

His work reflects little or no interest in contemporary Italian writers such as Ariosto or Tasso; perhaps the blending in their epics of fantasy and the supernatural was not to his taste; and in any case Kochanowski was not an epic poet. Instead, he learned certain technical matters from the Italians: the three-line stanza of Dante, the use of unrhymed eleven-syllabic lines in rhetorical tragedy, and lyricism from Petrarch.

Episodes and incidents in his personal life at Padua may have been incorporated in some of his songs and epigrams, to be discussed later. Although he does not appear to have personally known any educated or literary Italians, there was a fairly large colony of other young Poles at the university, with whom he may well have taken part in the riotous and even debauched pleasures of sixteenth-century Italy.

III   *Paris*

On his way home to Poland from his last stay in Italy, Kochanowski traveled through France and spent some three months there, late in 1558. But this visit is even more mysterious than his travels in Italy: we know nothing of whom he met or what he did, or even whether he knew French (he could, of course, communicate with educated men in Latin). Attempts to discover French "influences" in his work have met with little success.[5]

To be sure, Kochanowski claimed in one of his Latin elegies "I saw Ronsard," the leading poet of the Pléiade poets, who died in 1585. The Pléiade poets were animated by a common veneration for the writers of antiquity, and a desire to improve the quality of French poetry—ideals Kochanowski shared in regard to Polish poetry. But the claim cannot be substantiated, any more than Sir Philip Sidney's claim to have "seen Tasso." Most probably, we are hearing an echo of Ovid's claim to have seen Virgil.

CHAPTER 3

Court Poet

ALTHOUGH Kochanowski spent the next few years, perhaps even a decade, at various courts in Poland, he was never a "court poet" by nature. If he was at any time ambitious for success in court life (well-paid appointments and the like), he was disappointed. In any case, he lacked the "spirit of intrigue" and in society could appear "timid and surly,"[1] though we know him to have been a man who greatly prized companionship and the pleasures of love, music, and wine. Even the fact that he failed to compose the customary panegyric lament on the death of King Zygmunt I in 1572 suggests that he felt under no obligation to that monarch.

All writers, unless wealthy—and Kochanowski was not—require a certain amount of patronage early in their careers, and this was even more true in the sixteenth century than today. Patronage is never entirely or necessarily bad. In Kochanowski's period, nearly all artists who found a patron for themselves were at least assured of an audience able to appreciate their work.

However, poetry and the other arts in sixteenth-century Poland were less favored than they were in Italy, or even France and England. To be sure, the kings of Poland were cultivated, even enlightened. But the arts were not important (except, perhaps for architecture), despite the presence in Cracow of the Italian queen and her court. The great and wealthy magnates did not cultivate the arts as the Italian nobility often did. In any case, poetry was for the educated élite. Printing flourished, of course; but books were largely of a religious kind—tracts for or against Protestantism or Catholicism, prayer-books, hymnals, and the like.

Kochanowski cared little for public praise. He wrote comparatively few lengthy works, no prose of any consequence, and not all his poetry was printed during his lifetime. However, this manner of proceeding was not unusual in the sixteenth century, or even later. Sometimes a pious relative might make a posthumous collection and have the work printed as a memorial. But more often, poetry remained in manuscript and was circulated in copies among friends.

I A Game of Chess

Kochanowski's reluctance to have his work printed means that no reliable chronology can be established. For instance, the narrative poem (six hundred and two lines) *Szachy* (Game of Chess) seems to have been printed first between 1562 and 1566.

This pleasant little anecdote—it is scarcely more—is one of several books or poems on chess printed in Europe during the Renaissance: the most celebrated was a Latin poem by Giambattista Vida, and William Caxton's *The Game and Play of Chess* was one of the first books he printed (1475).

Vida's poem describes the invention of chess, and the first game played between Apollo and Mercury on Mount Olympus. Kochanowski abandoned the mythological apparatus, vitalizing the game and rendering it dramatic, even up to date. Kochanowski's game is played between two rivals for the hand of Anna, a Danish princess. The rivals, Fiedor and Borzuj, perhaps stand for Fiodor, a son of Ivan the Terrible, and a Scandinavian prince, contesting for the hand of King Zygmunt's daughter. The poem is set at the royal court in Denmark, though Kochanowski makes no attempt to provide "local color."

To Vida and his imitators, the game of chess is little more than a pretext for the display of their own erudition. Vida's game ends with the white king in checkmate to the black king, and later versions usually have this ending, though some writers did not trouble to give their games an ending at all. But Kochanowski concentrates on the final moves for the last two hundred lines.

After briefly setting the situation, Kochanowski describes the rules of the game and how the chessmen move (not very accurately). Fiedor plays white, Borzuj black. They place their pieces with some "hope" and "trepidation," and the game proceeds as though it were a real battle, with military terminology, until interrupted by suppertime. The two knights retire, the chessboard being placed under guard for the night. The Princess Anna, not knowing who will win her hand in marriage, anxiously makes her way into the room and examines the layout of the game, which is almost at an end (line 491 ff.), and weeps. The truth is that she loves Fiedor, but now she sees that "Fiedor already doubts the Princess, / While Borzuj supposes that he had already won for certain." Although Anna cannot alter the position of the chessmen, she turns Borzuj's Black Knight to face the White King, suggesting that Fiedor should capture it. When morning comes, Fiedor observes this slight change, follows the suggestion, and wins the game.[2]

Kochanowski's *Game of Chess* is essentially a mock-heroic poem like Vida's, in which elevated figures—kings, queens, bishops, knights—are reduced to the level of mere figures on a chessboard. But the plot can be related to the medieval romance, in which a typical situation was that of an old king placing various difficult or apparently impossible tasks to be surmounted by a young prince, or rival princes, before he will bestow the hand of his beautiful daughter upon one of them.

With its elegant, smooth couplets and diverting narrative line, Kochanowski's little book is regarded as one of the shorter masterpieces of the Polish Renaissance, and it was recently reprinted in Warsaw (1966) with appropriate woodcuts of the period.

II Concord

Another of Kochanowski's early works was *Zgoda* (Concord), first printed in 1564. Here, Kochanowski looks back to a favorite device of medieval writers, viz. personification, to express some of his own views on contemporary political matters.

Concord speaks:

I, Concord, who rule disputing planets,
And understand earth, water, fire in their elements,
I, guardian of republics, the health and defense of great cities,
Have come hither, though uninvited,

To you, O descendants of the Slavic Lech,
Pitying the misfortunes of a State so eminent.

Ja, Zgoda, która sporne planety sprawuję
    Ziemię, wodę, wiatr, ogień w żywiołach miarkuję,
Stróż rzeczypospolitych, zdrowie i obrona
    Miast wysokich—przyszłam tu, chocia nie proszona,
Do was, o potomkowie Lecha słowieńskiego,
    Litując niefortuny państwa tak zacnego.

She has come to reproach the Poles for the domestic dissension with which the Republic is beset and to protest that the churches are "full of blasphemy," the law courts "silent," and even Liberty is despaired of. Concord (and her creator) point accusingly at the manner in which the Polish gentry (Poland's largest and most influential social class, midway between the aristocracy and the peasants) were becoming tools in the hands of a small number of wealthy magnates. The latter spent vast sums of money bribing the gentry for their votes in the Sejm (House of Deputies).

Concord prophesies that Poland's hostile neighbors, Muscovy and Turkey to the east, Prussia to the west, are watching attentively for an opportunity to turn this inner discord in Poland to their own advantage. To support the argument, Concord quotes the fate of ancient Rome which, "though unconquered by Pyrrhus, Hannibal, Antiochus, the Gauls and the Teutons," nevertheless ceased to be a republic after the civil war between Caesar and Pompey in 48 B.C. She has more recent examples: only twenty years earlier, the Hungarian crown had been destroyed, also as a result of internal strife (the Turks captured Buda in 1541, taking advantage of the rivalry between the Hapsburg King Ferdinand and Duke Zapolyi).

Next, Concord declares she is distressed by the behavior of the Polish clergy, who "prefer to indulge themselves, / In unseemly pleasures and vain revelry," thus disgusting "simple folk" by their bad example. The disorder, even corruption, prevailing in the Catholic church in the first half of the sixteenth century (and earlier) had long been the target of satirists, in Poland as elsewhere. The Catholic church, after all, had provoked Martin Luther into demanding reforms in 1517, and from that movement burgeoned the various heretical sects—Calvinists, Arians, Puritans, the Czech Brothers and more. Kochanowski's slightly older contemporary, Mikołaj Rej, had satirically described the laxity of Polish rural clergy in a section of his long poem of 1543, entitled *A Brief Dispute between Three Persons, a Gentleman, a Village Mayor and a Priest* (Krótka rozprawa między trzema osobami . . .). The sale of indulgences, by means of which a person could ensure salvation for his soul, or at least the absolution of his sins, by paying money to the clergy, was particularly scandalous. To be sure, the Catholic church underwent considerable reforms in these respects after the Council of Trent in 1564, when the Jesuit order in particular initiated the Counter-Reformation.

Concord reverts to her earlier warnings against Poland's hostile neighbors, and points out that "the Republic has no defense, / Beset on every side by enemies." She concludes with an exhortation to her hearers: "Do you strive for social concord, / And restore the order that formerly prevailed." This call to revert to "ancient morality" echoes through Polish literature for the next three centuries, and more. Indeed, the call was one which had echoed through all the literatures of Europe ever since the Greek idylls of Theocritus in the second century B.C. But it had a special poignancy in Poland, as though writers through the years in some way foresaw the coming destruction of the Republic during the Partitions at the end of the eighteenth century, when Russia, Austro-Hungary, and Prussia brought about the end of the Polish State for over a century. The major writer of the Polish Age of Enlightenment, Ignacy Krasicki (1735–1801), emphasizes the need for a return to "old morality" in his novel *Pan Podstoli* (The Squire),[3] and Adam Mickiewicz celebrates the passing of the old order in his poem *Pan Tadeusz* (1834).[4] Both these poets admired Kochanowski's poetry.

III *The Mossy, Rude, Uncivil God*

In the period between writing *Concord* and *Satyr, albo Dziki mąż* (Satyr, or the Wild Man), Kochanowski's pessimistic view of the state of the Polish Republic evidently intensified. His pessimism was only too well founded: Zygmunt (to whom

Satyr is dedicated) only two years later resigned himself to
the loss of the town of Polotsk to the Muscovites; no reforms
inside Poland were initiated, and the king continued to vacillate
between Catholicism and Protestantism, while dissension ruled
among the heretics also.

Kochanowski continues to voice his profound concern with
the political and social conditions of sixteenth-century Poland.
The *Satyr* is an extended monologue, like Concord, with the
"wild man" himself speaking: "I am, as you see me . . . with
horns on my head, a face that's not beautiful, and hairy legs."
He is an example of the traditional creature to be found all
over Europe in medieval literature and art, who may in turn
derive from the Old Testament: "And Babylon . . . shall be as
when God overthrew Sodom and Gomorrah . . . and satyrs shall
dance there" (Isaiah 13:19–21), and from classical mythology,
in which the satyrs were part-human and part-goat deities,
who attended on the god Bacchus. He is also to be found in the
French Arthurian romances, in the epics of German minne-
singers, and in the writings of Cervantes and Spenser. A more
recent example of the species is Tarzan, though his affinity is
with apes, not goats.[5]

A wild man who appeared at the same time as Kochanowski's
satyr was figured in the poem *Lament of the Wild Man about
the Unfaithful World,* by Hans Sachs, the shoemaker of Nurem-
berg (1494–1576). The work was widely known. He laments the
evil ways of the corrupt world with somewhat monotonous
insistence for eighty lines or more. Both the Polish and the German satyrs are paragons of virtue, gentle and enlightened, above
ordinary mortals in being able to practice what they preach.
They are able to perform this unusual feat because the bane
of original sin does not extend to them, and they can therefore
be good without effort.

Kochanowski's satyr has deserted his native habitat ("the
deepest forests" of Poland) because the Poles are foolishly and
improvidently cutting down timber to export, thus capitalizing
in their greed on the country's natural resources. Like Concord,
so the Satyr harks back to "years ago," when "no one was
wealthy," and all Poles were prepared to "fight for seven years
without cease" to protect their homeland, if need be. Kocha-

nowski is here referring, through the satyr's mask, to the "execution of the laws," a legal statute which required all classes in Poland to undertake military service in defense of their country against attack by hostile neighbors. The statute was a source of discontent, because it fell most heavily on the peasants.

By this time, we have recognized the satyr's tone of voice; it is that of a politician making a speech, as politicians have been doing for centuries.[6] He gives his views, at the top of his voice and brooking no interruption, on matters ranging from national defense, and the reform of law-courts to the condition of the clergy and their delinquency. The rhetorical heat of the poem is intensified from time to time when he breaks off to demand of his audience: "Am I, or am I not, speaking the truth? Admit it yourselves!" or to declare "Brothers, I do not seek to enter into a dispute with you on Faith," or "I speak as I understand; he who has something better to say, let him speak up, / I will gladly listen."

Like many orators, the satyr leaves his most telling argument to the end of the monologue, when he utters a prophetic warning addressed directly to the king and to his fellow-countrymen. Internal dissension and lack of preparedness against attack can only lead to the destruction of the Republic. In this respect, he echoes Concord. But neither voice was listened to.

Kochanowski's satyr also brings up the question of the Polish peasantry, the most neglected of all social classes. Indeed, they remained serfs throughout most (though not all) of Poland until the middle of the nineteenth century. But other classes (the satyr adds) also required benevolent concern on the part of their betters: townsfolk, tradesmen, artisans, merchants, and craftsmen. The gentry should desist from their incessant preoccupation with profit, reform their often ruinous agricultural systems based on serfdom (Kochanowski did not call it that) and the exploitation of land, and curb their extravagances. Of course, there were benevolent and charitable gentry in sixteenth-century Poland, though we hear little of them.

Here, we are back in the Poland of Mikołaj Rej's debate *Brief Dispute* ... where the three characters reproach one another for their faults; the extravagance of the Gentleman with his passion for expensive clothes and foreign wines; the rapacity of the Priest; and the incompetence of the Village Mayor.

Neither *Concord* nor the *Satyr* is among Kochanowski's major achievements, though both demonstrate the technical skill he had acquired as early as the 1560's, in such matters as consistent use of feminine rhymes (two syllables) as opposed to masculine rhymes of one syllable. We never feel that Kochanowski wrote the second line of a couplet (the metrical pattern he most frequently used) simply for the sake of finding a rhyme. He also introduces the run-on line; in earlier writers, including Rej, the sense ended in a couplet. Kochanowski sometimes proceeds further, even in this early work, and was later to develop a highly sophisticated use of the device. Both feminine rhyming systems and run-on lines were admired and imitated by his followers, while the thematic influence of the "wild man" speaking his mind about the deplorable state of the Republic is attested by other literary satyrs who appear in Polish poetry into the eighteenth century.

Both poems are dramatic monologues, a genre which Kochanowski inherited from Horace, though he did not practice them again, except in the play *Odprawa posłów greckich* (Dismissal of the Grecian Envoys) where their function is somewhat different. He knew the peculiar difficulties which arise in using the form. The writer must provide his hearers with background information, but not list facts perfectly obvious to the person he is supposed to be addressing through the mask. That Kochanowski succeeded in this difficult genre is a measure of his rapidly developing mastery of technique, as is the fact that both poems are reprinted and read at the present day.

IV The Banner

Kochanowski's work, especially during the early "court" period of his life, contains frequent references to Poland's relations with Muscovy and Prussia. He was not by any means a poet of peace, and in this respect differs from Ronsard, who detested "military glory." Thus, in addition to the two dramatic monologues already described, with their warnings against the military power of Muscovy, Kochanowski also wrote a relatively short narrative poem *Proporzec, albo Hołd pruski* (The Banner, or Prussian Homage) to celebrate the historic occasion when King Zygmunt II August graciously deigned to accept Prince Albrecht II of Prussia's act of homage and oath of allegiance to the Polish crown in 1569.

Dedicated to the Polish commander-in-chief and Palatine of Ruthenia, Jerzy Jazlowiecki, the poem brings to mind, and may well have served as the inspiration for, Jan Matejko's celebrated painting of the scene, entitled "Prussian Homage" (1881). This is by no means the only occasion on which a painter has been drawn to illustrating a work of literature; several of Matejko's panoramic historical canvasses drew their inspiration from the vast historical novels of Henryk Sienkiewicz, his contemporary.[7]

In the poem, Kochanowski depicts the Polish king seated on his throne "in splendid attire, and a golden crown," holding a "golden crown and sceptre." Prince Albrecht steps forward to pay homage and vow to "keep faith." After this, the king hands Albrecht the banner, which is "all painted with costly colors, / Great, splendid, gorgeous." When unfurled, it reveals "kings, armies, palatines, rivers, cities, and towns." Kochanowski enumerates details, which include the capture of Danzig by the Poles in 1308, the marriage of King Kazimierz the Great to Aldona, daughter of a Lithuanian prince, and the hostilities between Poles and their many traditional enemies—Germans, Prussians, Muscovites, and Tartars. The unfurling of the banner is accompanied by the sound of trumpets and the beating of drums; and the poem ends with all the company proceeding to a banquet, by which Kochanowski expresses the hope that the Union between Poland and Lithuania remains firm.

The act of union (1569), which *The Banner* celebrates, and which brought about the merger of Poland and Lithuania, was a remarkable political achievement, comparable to the act of union between England and Scotland in 1605. The result was to form a vast territory stretching from the Baltic Sea to the Dniester River, which lasted until the Partitions, when the region became a province of the Russian Empire. The area was multilingual and multireligious; Catholic Poland tolerated not only Jews and heretical sects such as the Arians, Lutherans, and

Calvinists, but also the Greek Orthodox faith, to which the Lithuanians and Ruthenians adhered. Some aristocratic Polish families in the area even became Moslems, and mosques are to be seen to this day in (for instance) the Białystok area. Lithuania was to be the birthplace of Poland's national poet, Adam Mickiewicz (1798–1854); all his major works are permeated with a lifelong devotion to the Lithuanian countryside and the capital, Wilno (*Forefathers Eve, Pan Tadeusz*), and even his *Crimean Sonnets* hark back to Mickiewicz's homeland.

Other minor poems of a political nature which Kochanowski composed at various times include the *Jezda do Moskwy* (Expedition to Muscovy), written to celebrate the capture of Polotsk in 1579, but not printed until 1583; this indicates that Kochanowski felt under an obligation to write panegyrics throughout his life (it was a year before his death). The poem is dedicated to Prince Krzysztof Radziwiłł. Its tone is elevated; stiff with classical references, this poem is the nearest Kochanowski ever came to an epic, although it is only four hundred and ten lines long.

Another early poem is *Muza* (The Muse), in which a note of disillusionment sounds:

I sing to myself and the Muses. For who in the world
Would wish to rejoice his heart with my songs?
. . . For what advantage is there to rhymes, except empty sound?
But he who has money, has everything in his grasp . . .
While the poet, devoid of listeners, plays behind the fence.

Sobie śpiewam a Muzom. Bo kto jest na ziemi,
    Co by serce ucieszyć chcial pieśniami memi?
    Bo z rymów co za korzyść krom próznego dzwięku?
    Ale kto ma pieniądze, ten ma wszytko w ręku . . .
    A poeta, słuchaczów prózny, gra za płotem.

In the poem, Kochanowski affirms his vocation as a poet, defining his art as "purification and initiation into knowledge and virtue." Poetry, not the poet's patron, bestows glory on him and the heroes in whose honor he sings—a familiar idea in classical antiquity, e.g., Horace's ode IV, ix "Ne forte credas interitura," later adopted by poets of the Renaissance, including

Ronsard. But Kochanowski is saluting the epic Horace of the Roman odes, not the Bacchic.

V *Divine Poetry*

The Bible was an inexhaustible source book for poets, particularly when the great "pagan" writers began to be regarded with increasing suspicion by the Church. Even classical mythology was suspect. Consequently, sixteenth-century poets seeking to try their hand at narrative poems or drama often turned to the Bible for subjects. Mikołaj Rej wrote his drama *Żywot Józefa* (Life of Joseph), 1545, based on the Old Testament story of Joseph and the wife of Potiphar, though the play was not produced. Numerous other instances occur elsewhere in Europe; the French poet du Bartas transformed the story of Judith into a narrative poem, and the Scots poet George Buchanan used Biblical stories to mirror contemporary events (his Herod, John the Baptist, and Herodias served as masks for Henry VIII, Sir Thomas More, and Ann Boleyn), and there were many Italian examples of the genre also.

Kochanowski drew on the Old Testament for one of his earliest poems to be printed, "Pieśń o potopie" (Song about the Deluge, *ca.* 1558), which was later incorporated, slightly revised, in the collection of his *Songs*. Kochanowski summarizes the six weeks of Noah's flood, preceded by "unseasonable rains" causing waters to "roar from the mountains, and the foamy river Wilia / Bursts its banks." The last stanza, addressed to the poet's ever-present lute, urges the instrument to "tell us to sit by a warm chimneypiece / Until the bad weather passes." The reference to Horace's ode I, ii—"We saw the yellow Tiber, waves driven / Raging back from its Etruscan bank . . ." is, of course, conscious—except that Horace's version of the Deluge is entirely pagan, while Kochanowski's derives from Holy Writ.

In 1562, Kochanowski again drew on the Old Testament, this time to versify the tale of Susanna and the Elders (*Zuzanna*). Although the entire story was regarded by Protestants as apocryphal, it appeared in the Vulgate, so Catholic dogma accepted it. But, to complicate matters somewhat, Kochanowski dedicated the poem to Mikołaj Radziwiłł, patron of Calvinists

in Lithuania. But this does not mean that Kochanowski himself was drawn to Calvinism on the one hand, or Catholicism
on the other.

The tale of the virtuous Susanna and the wicked Elders, who
gaze sinfully at her while she is bathing, gave many writers
and artists the opportunity to indulge their various tastes; some
medieval romances drew on the plot for its narrative interest.
In Poland, a now forgotten neo-Latin poet, Jeremi Wojnoski,
published his *Historia Susannae* only five years later than Kochanowski's appeared. The Polish Baroque poet, Sebastian Grabowiecki, composed a poem included in his *Setniki* (Centuries)
of 1590 (no. x). Other versions included the English *Rewarde
of Wickednesse* (1574) by Richard Robinson, where the Elders
are depicted in the "stinking Stygian pitte" of Hell, along with
other wicked persons including Helen of Troy and Pope Alexander VI. The tale reappears in Greene's *Mirror of Modesty*
(1584). These versions all have a moralizing function.[8]

In the Baroque period, painters found the story appealing,
though now it was the sensual aspect of the incident which
appealed; Tintoretto, Veronese, van Dyck, Rubens, and Rem-
brandt all painted the beautiful Susanna bathing, while the
Elders watch. To Kochanowski, of course, the incident was of
interest because of its moral; he dwells on the moral problem
of virtue by exploring Susanna's character and feelings; the Old
Testament version provided no motivations for the characters
or their "psychology," and Kochanowski had to invent these.
So, for instance, he provides an account (lines 107 ff.) of the
night spent by Susanna after the Elders have threatened to
expose her (falsely) for taking a lover. This section, in which
Susanna weeps, curses Fortune (a figure who appears throughout Kochanowski's poetry), and resolves to destroy herself, does
not occur in the Apocrypha. Her extended speeches on Virtue
are also Kochanowski's own invention, deriving from Stoic
doctrines widely held during the Renaissance to the effect that
"Virtue is its own reward"—another theme to which Kochanowski continually returned and sometimes questioned.

By these and other alterations and additions to the Biblical
text, Kochanowski greatly intensified the secular and moralistic
nature of the poem. On the other hand, he does not refer to

Susanna's strictly Mosaic upbringing, stressed in the Bible: and when Susanna is accused of committing adultery, she hesitates before replying to the charge; martyrs in the Bible never hesitate, indeed they greet martyrdom with exultation.

Kochanowski's narrative takes place in ancient Babylon, where Susanna lives with her "virtuous and prosperous spouse," Joachim. Susanna herself is "marvellously fair, young and comely." Kochanowski describes their household and draws our attention at the outset to an alabaster fountain in their garden. This reference is an adroit touch of narrative technique, as the fountain later plays an important role in the development of the plot.

Now the Elders appear; they are frequent visitors to the house of Joachim, and both allow themselves to be "led astray" by Susanna's beauty. As she bathes in the fountain, they declare their lust; she repulses their advances, and they threaten to accuse her of committing adultery. In reply to Susanna's cry, servants appear, but the Elders persist in their accusations. Alone that night, Susanna reflects on her plight in a long tirade reminiscent of those uttered by heroines in classical tragedy.

Next morning Susanna is accused before judges. She protests her innocence, and "God takes mercy upon her," by sending the prophet Daniel to confound the Elders. The virtuous Susanna is spared, and Kochanowski points out that "the wicked find no refuge from His vengeance."

This artless little tale was more familiar to Kochanowski's contemporaries than to us, and for this reason Kochanowski clearly saw the necessity for adding his own freshness to it. As the late Professor Borowy pointed out, the poem contains turns of phrase which could hardly have been composed by any other poet but Kochanowski, e.g., "Then day departed, night took its place, / Eclipsing all earth and sky with its wings" (lines 101–102)[9] (A wtym dzień zszedł, noc na jego miejsce nastąpiła, / Swymi skrzydły wszytkę ziemię i niebo zaćmiła). At first, this couplet is not particularly striking; but Kochanowski did not aim to be striking. Unlike the Baroque poets of the seventeenth century, with their often grotesque, even bizarre imagery, "conceits . . . exaggerated metaphors and graphomania" (Dr. Johnson's celebrated phrase), Kochanowski achieved his finest effects by cultivating simplicity. In Kochanowski's poetry, the

total effect is what counts, not the single line or image. Then
again, Kochanowski's handling of everyday occurrences—dusk,
dawn, the changing seasons of the year, even the weather—
permeates his work with its essentially human tone.

VI *"The Song"*

When *Susanna* was first printed in 1564, the volume also contained what was to become one of Kochanowski's best-known
and loved poems: "Czego chcesz od nas, Panie..." (What
would You wish of us, O Lord...), which are its opening
words. Kochanowski called it simply "Pieśń" (Song). The
poem's tone is biblical, and indeed foreshadows Kochanowski's
work in the 1570's on the Psalms (see next chapter). Its apparent simplicity has led translators to render it in other languages,
two of which follow: comparisons would be odious, but each
version has its own felicities and lapses.

After the gifts you have lavished, Lord, what would you have?
What fit return shall we find for your infinite love?
The church cannot contain you—you are everywhere,
Filling the depths, the sea, the earth, the endless air.

Oh, I am sure you need no gold; it's yours alone
To give, as are all the things man calls his own.
So we will pay homage with a grateful heart, my Lord,
Since that is the worthiest gift we can afford.

Great Lord of the World, it was you who raised the sky,
Embroidering gold stars upon its tapestry;
You who took this formless earth, built a foundation,
And clothed its grim nakedness with vegetation.

At your command, the wild sea stops at the shore,
Leaps to the level boundaries, and leaps no more;
But faithful rivers serve you, bringing fruits and flowers,
As day and night attend to their appointed hours.

Fair Spring presents you with the flowers of the heath;
For your sake haughty Summer wears a floral wreath;
Sweet Autumn loads your store with fruit and wine
That gracious Winter may, when she awakens, dine.

Although the rose is withered by your strength, the rain
With gentle fingers raises up a stalwart grain.
And just as the beast finds in your hand much food,
We too get life from you, and all things good.

May you be happy, gracious Lord, Ruler and Giver.
Your grace, your goodness will never perish—never!
Protect as you will these poor wards of the land,
And as for me, let me be governed by your hand.

> (Translated by A. and Gerald Darring)

Another version, also metrical and rhymed, of the same text:

What do you want of us, great God, who gives
Limitless favor to each thing that lives?
The Church will not contain you, you, entire
In every inch of water, land and fire.

Riches is [*sic*] useless since to you alone
Belongs each jewel that man thinks his own.
A grateful heart, great God, is all that can
Be offered to you by poor things like man.

You built the sky, embroidered galaxies
And sketched foundations so that from them rise
Perimeters too huge for men to trace;
Earth's nakedness you covered with green grace.

Great God of all the world, the sea obeys
Your vast commands and keeps to its set ways.
The rivers richen. Day knows when to dawn.
Night and the twilight linger and are gone.

The Spring brings garlands and the Summer wears
A crown of wheat like girls who dance at fairs,
Autumn dispenses apples, wine and mirth,
Then Winter sluggishly prepares the earth.

At night your gardeners spray each plant with dew.
By day your rain wakes withering plants anew.
The beasts eat at your hand and every sense
Is nourished by you with munificence.

Immortal God, grace most continual,
Be praised for ever. Keep us where we shall
Best serve your purpose, now and when we die
Safe in the shadow of your wings that fly.

(Translated by Jerzy Peterkiewicz and Burns Singer)

Czego chcesz od nas, Panie, za Twe hojne dary?
Czego za dobrodziejstwa, którym nie masz miary?
Kościół Cię nie ogarnie, wszędy pełno Ciebie,
I w otłanach, i w morzu, na ziemi, na niebie.

Złota też, wiem, nie pragniesz, bo to wszytko Twoje,
Cokołwiek na tym świecie człowiek mieni swoje.
Wdzięcznym Cię tedy sercem, Panie, wyznawamy,
Bo nad to przystojniejszej ofiary nie mamy.

Tyś pan wszytkiego świata, Tyś niebo zbudował
I złotymi gwiazdami ślicznieś uhaftował;
Tyś fundament założył nieobeszłej ziemi
I przykryłeś jej nagość zioły rozlicznemi.

Za Twoim rozkazaniem w brzegach morze stoi,
A zamierzonych granic przeskoczyć się boi;
Rzeki wód nieprzebranych wielką hojność mają,
Biały dzień, a noc ciemna swoje czasy znają.

Tobie k'woli rozliczne kwiatki Wiosna rodzi,
Tobie k'woli w kłosianym wieńcu Lato chodzi.
Wino Jesień i jabłka rozmaite dawa,
Potym do gotowego gnuśna Zima wstawa.

Z Twej łaski nocna rosa na mdłe zioła padnie,
A zagorzałe zboża deszcz ożywia snadnie;
Z Twoich rąk wszelkie źwierzę patrza swej żywności,
A Ty każdego żywisz z Twej szczodrobliwości.

Bądź na wieki pochwalon, nieśmiertelny Panie!
Twoja łaska, Twa dobroć nigdy nie ustanie.
Chowaj nas, póki raczysz, na tej niskiej ziemi;
Jedno zawżdy niech będziem pod skrzydłami Twemi!

Kochanowski's tone of restraint in the poem might be mistaken
for coldness or lack of feeling, especially by readers accustomed

to the more "passionate" writings of, say, the Romantics. But the restraint is what gives "The Song" its impressive nobility. The tone is subdued, rather than exalted; we find no unexpected turns of phrase, or of versification. Kochanowski is, of course, reshaping traditional beliefs and using traditional language. But the beliefs and language were also his own.

"The Song" also gives a picture of the world, built according to and functioning by harmony, that concept so valued by Renaissance humanists; the harmony is reflected in the ordered passing of the seasons of the year. Later, in the *Laments*, Kochanowski describes the collapse of this harmonious world-picture, as he goes through a spiritual crisis brought about by a personal tragedy in his life.

After Kochanowski's Psalms (see next chapter), "The Song" was his most frequently translated poem; a German version was printed in Leszno (1639), later in Amsterdam and Berlin. A Czech version, existing among the folk in Bohemia, was attributed by nineteenth-century ethnographers to Moravian folklore, where it probably arrived through a Protestant hymnbook.[10]

CHAPTER 4

"Songs of the City of God"

K OCHANOWSKI spent almost a decade rendering the *Book of Psalms* into Polish. First printed in 1575 or 1578, his psalms went into numerous editions. Indeed, for over a century, the Psalms remained his best-loved work. Set to music, they continue to be sung in Polish churches, both Catholic and Protestant, to the present day. In quantity, they amount to almost a third of Kochanowski's total output in Polish.

As with most of Kochanowski's poetry, we know little about the circumstances under which he worked on the immense task (one hundred and fifty psalms altogether, divided into five parts). As early as 1571 he wrote to a friend, Stanisław Fogelweder, one of King Zygmunt II's secretaries, that he hoped to have thirty psalms ready "for the king," who, however, died the next year.

The work has been described as his "poetical laboratory," in which he experimented with a great variety of stanza patterns, meters, rhymes, and vocabulary.[1] But what prompted Kochanowski the humanist to choose the Psalms for translation? With their often high-flown songs of praise, thanksgiving, supplication and imprecation, with audacious, sometimes bizarre imagery, echoing with the name of forgotten desert tribes and containing prophecies and visions—the Psalms were poetry of a kind far removed from Renaissance ideals of poetry. Of course, he knew that the Book of Psalms had a special position among all existing collections of prayers; but he certainly did not know that some parts of the collection date from 1000 B.C. and that it was completed probably by the third century B.C. From that time, the Psalms have been in uninterrupted use.[2] This is a unique case; many prayers from other cults, some even older than the Psalms, are known to us; but they are museum pieces, relics of a dead past, addressed to deities long forgotten by man. But the Psalms continue to live as expressions of faith and worship.

Kochanowski never expressed his views on the Psalms, but like many of his contemporaries, from Clément Marot to Sir Philip Sidney, he knew the Psalms were *poems*—the most significant and influential collection of religious poems ever made; and that they must be read as poetry if they are to be understood. Rightly, they have been described as a "great organ of human sentiment, upon whose stops the Holy Spirit varies the moods of a divine melody."[3] Statements like this suggest that the key words in referring to the Psalms are "poems" and "poetry," the aspect which attracted Renaissance poets to rendering them in the vernacular languages. Indeed, the Psalms constituted a source of poetic inspiration for dozens of writers, in much the same way that the entire Bible had provided medieval writers with sources for countless allegories, of which twentieth-century man is almost totally ignorant. Moreover, the learned knew that the Psalms had originally been composed for chanting, not silent reading.

Kochanowski approached his task as a humanist, not as a theologian or composer of a prayer book. As his poetry demonstrates, he was supremely confident of the value of poetry in human life. Medieval scholasticism had no place in his work. His poetry does not concern itself with dogma. God, or the Supreme Being as Kochanowski sometimes calls Him, was not the jealous figure of dread of the Old Testament, but (as witness the "Song" already described) a Being whom man venerates and worships. But, like his contemporary Erasmus of Rotterdam, whose writings Kochanowski knew, he was reluctant to investigate the "mysteries of God," such attempts being beyond the competence of man.[4]

I *The Psalms in Translation*

For many centuries, the Psalms were the most frequently translated book of the Old Testament. The earliest was in Gothic (fourth century A.D.), followed by an Anglo-Saxon metrical version and the Oxford Psalter. Latin versions were made, the best-known being that of the Scot George Buchanan (1566), which Kochanowski knew and which he imitated with regard to metrical variety.

In Poland, renderings of the Book of Psalms in the vernacular did not appear until the end of the fourteenth century (the Floriański and Puławy psalters, which are, of course, in manuscript copies). Three versions were made in the sixteenth century before that of Kochanowski: one, anonymous, in 1532, that of W. Wróbel in 1535, and Mikołaj Rej's in 1546. All are in prose, and in any case all these writers were inspired more by piety than by poetry.

The Psalms were first established as poetry in a vernacular language by Clément Marot, the Pléiade poet, with his *Psaulmes de Davide* of 1541. Marot's versions were much admired, especially in England, where Sir Thomas Wyatt published the first poetic paraphrase of the *Seven Penitential Psalms* (1549). He proceeded in 1562 to print the *Whole Booke of Psalms*, which was incorporated into the English church services, and frequently reprinted. However, the most "poetic" English rendering of the Psalms is generally conceded to be that of Sir Philip Sidney, completed after his death by Mary, Countess of Pembroke, his sister.[5] Sidney's versions constituted an entire school of English versification, just as Kochanowski's in Polish. Both writers demonstrated in their respective languages a remarkable ability to integrate meaning with stanza form, and both clearly thought in terms of form rather than content.

Sidney's *Psalms* were not printed until the nineteenth century, but the work was circulated in a large number of manuscript copies—like so much poetry, including some of Kochanowski's—and was well known to John Donne, among others.

Though Kochanowski and Sidney were contemporaries, they obviously did not know each other's work (even though Sidney paid a brief visit to Poland in the 1570's).[6] Yet, in addition to the general similarities noted above, both versions share certain stylistic traits. Both poets knew that the Psalms had originally been composed in "measured verse," which justified poetic renderings, as distinct from the prose of the other books of the Old Testament. Indeed, this fact was a prime difficulty when poets set about versifying the Psalms. As they were intended for chanting, or singing, a particularly rich, even orotund effect was required, marked by strength, fullness, and richness. Kochanowski achieved this style in several ways—through epithets of various kinds in particular. The metrical patterns were also carefully chosen; in the "historical narrative" Psalms, such as no. 78, giving an account of the Exodus and crossing of the Red Sea, Kochanowski used thirteen-syllabic lines—a meter that became traditional in Polish poetry when an elevated or epic style was called for. Sidney also chose his meters carefully, and John Dryden was later to remark on the "majesty, perfection and solidity" of the English version of the same Psalm.

II   *Epithets*

A feature of the style of the Old Testament as a whole is the frequent use of emphatic negatives, in sharp contrast to the teachings of Christ which are expressed as positives. Kochanowski's Psalms also abound in negatives, usually epithets describing God, who is said to be "immeasurable" (niezmierzony) in Psalms 13, 54, 60, 71, 90, 97, and 130; elsewhere He is "infinite" (nieprzeżyty), "unconquered" (niezwalczony), "immortal" (nieśmiertelny), "unalterable" (nieodmieniony), "incomprehensible" (niepojęty), and so forth. Professor Julian Krzyżanowski lists over sixty negative epithets used by Kochanowski, most now obsolete (not all are from the Psalms, however).[7] The effect of such epithets used frequently is to stress the remoteness of the Old Testament God.

But negative epithets are not used exclusively in describing God: we find other examples, such as "inexpressible mercy" (niewyslowione milosierdzie), "irreproachable judge" (sędzia nienagoniony), "inescapable bow" (łuk nieuchroniony), and others. Sidney shared this predilection with Kochanowski, writing "undefiled hartes," "undying rhymes," "unworn wheels," "unstedfast change," "unthralled," and the like. Both poets knew that Aristotle had recommended elevating a description in epic poetry by listing attributes the person or thing described did *not* possess.

Another kind of epithet, also deriving from classical epic poetry, was the compound, much favored by poets of the

Renaissance. Ronsard, for instance, believed the duty of patriotic French poets was to "manufacture new words on the pattern of Greek and Latin originals ... thereby making their own language the equal of foreign tongues."[8] English poets imitated the fashion; Spenser writes "sea-shouldering whales," Sidney used "scorne-gold hair" and "life-giving lights." Kochanowski likewise coins "swift-feathered bird" (ptak prędkopióry), "sea-flying vessels" (okręty morzolotne), "Thou the many-powerful" (Ty wielowładny), "all-fertile year" (rok wszytkorodny), and "high-flying sun" (słońce gorolotne). Such inventions were a novelty in Polish poetry of the sixteenth century, but were soon adopted by other writers (as were other of Kochanowski's innovations in prosody and vocabulary). The compound epithet remains a feature of Polish poetry until the end of the Age of Enlightenment (1796).

A third sort of epithet characteristic of Kochanowski's Psalms and indeed much of his poetry as a whole is best described as "neutral," not drawing attention to itself. The sky is "lofty" (wysoki), slavery "heavy" (ciężka), weeping "inconsolable" (nieutulony), tyrants "cruel" (okrutni), a harp "gilded" (złocona), and gifts "generous" (szczodre). As with the compound epithets, the neutral epithets, too, were used frequently in eighteenth-century Polish poetry (as they were by English contemporaries, including Alexander Pope). The effect was always to neutralize or "dampen" too ebullient lines. As with other stylistic devices, the eighteenth-century usage was yet another way of reacting against the stylistic excesses of the Baroque.

Kochanowski uses nearly five hundred epithets of various kinds in his Psalms, of which one hundred and thirty do not occur elsewhere in his other poetry.[9] This suggests he was using them for special effects of grandeur, cultivating archaisms for the purpose, and using elevated turns of speech, without the colloquialisms so frequent in the Polish epigrams.

III *Synonyms*

Yet another characteristic feature of Kochanowski's style in the Psalms (shared by Sidney) was the copious use of synonyms, or near synonyms, usually in groups of three. A few examples out of many must suffice: "the complaints of wretched people / And inconsolable weeping, and heavy sighing" (ludzi nędznych narzekanie / I płacz nieutulony, i ciężkie wzdychanie), "the sentences of the Lord are all rightful, /All eternal / all just" (Wyroki Pańskie wszytki są prawdziwe, / Wszytki stateczne, wszytki sprawiedliwe), "Defend me from a cruel sword, mad dogs, fierce lions" (Obroń ... szabli okrutnej, psom wścieklym lwom śrogim), "He gathers, collects, piles up" (Zbiera, gromadzi, skupuje), "In a dry, waterless, parched land" (W suchej, bezwodnej, upragnionej ziemi). In Sidney, we encounter such groups as "with lute, and harp, and voice," "my reliefe, my aide, my comfort," "broken, hewn, disperst," "my grace, my guard, my fort," "rape, murther, violence," "my reproach, my blot, my blame." To be sure, both Kochanowski and Sidney may have introduced such tricolons (groups of three words or phrases) for metrical purposes or for rhyme; even so, they also indicate a new feeling for the wealth of their own vernaculars.

IV   *Polish Elements*

As might be expected, Kochanowski occasionally saw fit in his version of the Psalms to make a few small alterations, to make the texts sound somewhat less strange to his Polish readers by introducing purely Polish elements. He did not go as far as Górnicki had done a few years earlier in his *Polish Courtier,* but his restraint was due to the fact that the Psalms were, after all, Holy Writ, and therefore unusual closeness to the original was essential. *The Courtier* was a secular book, and the text could be altered, especially to make it more accessible to what Górnicki called "the domestic Pole" (Polak domowy).

So Kochanowski makes only a few minor changes; the Biblical "bulls of Bashan" become wolves, the "cedars of Lebanon" appear as oak trees, and the birds of the Psalmist are defined as "sparrows." Similarly, wild goats become the more familiar roe deer, though Kochanowski retains camels, and saw no need to alter the phrase "as for the stork, the fir trees are her dwelling-place," since both bird and tree were familiar.

V *Reception*

In Poland, other poets started drawing on Kochanowski's *Psalms*, especially for vocabulary and new stanza forms. Sebastian Grabowiecki, a contemporary of Kochanowski, was clearly familiar with his *Psalms*, as witness Grabowiecki's *Setniki* (Centuries, 1590). Baroque poets of the seventeenth century drew on them, producing their own versions (e.g., Wespazjan Kochowski's *Psalmodia polska* [Polish Psalmodia, 1695], in "poetic prose"). Wacław Rzewuski published *Seven Penitential Psalms* in 1773, and other poets of the Age of Enlightenment who expressed their indebtedness in various ways ranged from Adam Naruszewicz to Franciszek Karpiński[10] and Franciszek Kniaźniń.[11] Indeed, the last-named admitted in a footnote to his version of Psalm 125 that "the final stanza is Jan Kochanowski's, so beautiful and felicitous that I have ventured to pin it to my translation, like a rosebud to a garland, with all the respect due to him."

But the fame of Kochanowski's *Psalms* was by no means restricted to Poland and the Polish language; they were known in Russia, where Simeon Polotskij's version (1680) was condemned by the Greek Orthodox Patriarch as heretical, since it was based on Kochanowski's (presumably) Catholic text.[12] In Bohemia, Jan Comenius knew them, as did poets in Serbia; they were also read in non-Slavic countries of Eastern Europe—Hungary, Lithuania, and Rumania. The Silesian poet Martin Opitz, writing in German, may owe some of his Psalms (1637) to Kochanowski's, which were also set to music by German composers. Many appear also in Prussian hymnbooks of the seventeenth century.[13]

In all these countries, Kochanowski's *Psalms* demonstrated that a vernacular language was a suitable medium for the most elevated poetry. In this way, Kochanowski's work contributed to the upsurge of national awareness which appeared all over Europe in the sixteenth century.

CHAPTER 5

Dismissal of the Grecian Envoys

IN January 1578, Kochanowski's only play, *Odprawa posłów greckich* (Dismissal of the Grecian Envoys), was performed at the festivities held during the marriage of Krystyna Radziwiłł to the magnate Jan Zamoyski (who also commissioned the writing of the play). This is the only secular drama of the sixteenth century to have been occasionally revived; there was a television performance in Warsaw a year or two ago. However, the history of the Polish theater began as early as the twelfth century, with performances of liturgical drama, usually given in connection with the calendar of the Catholic church—Easter, Christmas, Corpus Christi, or saints' days. They staged stories from the Bible, a book not commonly available—and these performances were used as opportunities for delivering sermons to the populace inside churches, or in cemeteries, or marketplaces, as was the case all over Western Europe in the Middle Ages. The actors were drawn from religious fraternities, or trade guilds, or schools and colleges. No texts have survived from before the sixteenth century, though the dramas were presumably given in Polish, and church documents (uchwały synodów) indicate that the performances sometimes terminated in coarse horseplay and drunkenness.

Secular drama in sixteenth-century Poland, as elsewhere in Europe, had its origins in the Italian Cinquecento, when writers used the dramas of classical antiquity as their models, both for themes and production. This kind of drama was cultivated at the royal court of Zygmunt I in Cracow. A play was presented there as early as 1510, though neither title nor text has survived. In 1522, *The Judgment of Paris* (in Latin) by the German humanist Jacob Locher was presented, and the text printed for the occasion. A Polish version was made and evidently aroused much interest, as four editions were printed within the next twenty years.

In addition to the Italian elements at the court, there were also academic elements from Cracow Academy. Stanisław of Łowicz, a member of the academy, produced *The Judgment of Paris*, and students of the academy performed in it. They had no stage or even theater proper, and the performance probably took place in Wawel castle. The play looks back to classical antiquity, being divided into three acts by two farcical *intermediae*, modeled on those of the Roman playwright Plautus, which provided opportunities for music, singing, and dancing, in which the court delighted.

However, there is no record of any other productions until Bona Sforza brought actors of the *commedia dell'arte* (impromptu comedies, featuring Harlequin, Columbine, and other traditional figures) to Cracow in the 1540's. One reason for the apparent decline of interest in matters theatrical was the decline of the Cracow Academy, dating from the mid-1530's. Also, Bona Sforza left Poland in 1557.

A secular play which has survived was the *Tragedia żebracza* (Beggar's Tragedy), printed in 1551. Neither the court nor the academy was associated with this farcical account of the wedding celebrations of professional beggars, held in a tavern and ending with the parodied proceedings of a law court. Only a few pages of the Polish text survive, but it was translated at the time in Czech and has been reconstructed on the basis of that version. The play was popular, and is referred to in the early seventeenth century.

Gradually Latin plays were translated into Polish and performed, though there were still no theaters. Favorite authors were Terence (died 159 B.C.) and Plautus (died 184 B.C.). What the public liked, of course, was the farcical action and coarse personages—drunken soldiers, whores, and the like. However, these Latin plays were pagan, and the Church could not approve of them. We have already noticed, in describing Kochanowski's "divine poem" *Susanna*, that this reaction against the pagan authors was widespread in sixteenth-century Europe.

Another example of "divine drama" in sixteenth-century Poland was the *Historia o chwalebnym zmartwychstaniu Pańs-*

kim (Tale of the Glorious Resurrection of Our Lord) of 1551; it is a "mystery play" and may well be considerably older than its date of printing. The text is furnished with production notes. The play itself was revived with success at the National Theater in Warsaw in 1963, then acclaimed by critics and audiences alike when the production toured Western Europe the following year. Picturesque and primitive, the *Tale* is a characteristically medieval mystery play, with its alternation of elevated and coarse, even farcical, scenes.

I *Aristocratic Patronage*

Kochanowski had already composed much of the *Dismissal of the Grecian Envoys* when Zamoyski commissioned it, so that although short (just over six hundred lines), the play was not hastily written for the occasion. The play, when printed, was prefaced by a letter of dedication to "My gracious lord" Jan Zamoyski, in which Kochanowski declares:

Only yesterday did I receive both letters which your lordship wrote to me about this tragedy. But, as I did not know of these letters earlier, I had supposed that, like the delays of our times, so too my tragedy was to be delayed, or used to feed moths, or serve as wrapping paper for an apothecary. When I read your lordship's letters, there was no time for corrections, all had to be used for copying. Be this as it may, and I think it a trifle merely, and your lordship will say the same, I send it to you the more boldly as there is nothing else to send though I told your lordship in advance that the thing was not according to the rules, for I am no master of them. Other things also are not to our ears. There are, also, three choruses, the third seeming to imitate Greek choruses . . . and I do not know how it will sound in Polish. But your lordship shall be the arbiter. . . .

Czarnolas, the twenty-second of December, 1577.

We cannot take Kochanowski's disparaging remarks about his own play too seriously, but the references to the three choruses in the play reveal Kochanowski's awareness of their originality, which will be remarked upon in due course.

The *Dismissal* is an entirely different work from those previously mentioned here; it is in Polish, not Latin, and the production which was given in the presence of King Stefan Batory as well as the aristocratic married pair, was suitably aristocratic too, all the parts being played by "noble young persons," not students. Nevertheless, Kochanowski went back to classical antiquity for his plot, dramatizing an episode from Homer's *Iliad*—the captivity of the Grecian Helen in Troy by Alexander, also known as Paris. (*The Judgment of Paris* mentioned earlier is a different legend entirely.) The tale had been retold many times, appearing in a sixteenth-century version known as *The History of the Destruction of the City of Troy* that was widely read all over Europe.[1] This work looks back to the twelfth-century *Romance of Troy*, which contributed largely to the revival of interest in classical history and legend.

The History of the Destruction was an immense work of some thirty thousand lines, which still remains one of the most remarkable of the many French romances on classical subjects. The subject matter is the Trojans' expedition to Greece and the abduction of the beautiful Helen, who is taken back to Troy and held for ransom. In most versions, the Trojans are the villains, but here they are shown as the innocent party, the Greeks as brutal aggressors. Of course, Virgil's *Aeneid* helped form the tradition that the Trojans were a virtuous and patriotic nation—Aeneas in the poem is himself a descendant of the Trojans and at the same time the legendary founder of Rome.

Even though Kochanowski drew on this antiquated model for his plot, he treated it in a way that was thoroughly contemporary. By now, the "divine drama" of the late Middle Ages was old-fashioned. Kochanowski therefore turned to a new kind of drama already flourishing in Italy and elsewhere, namely the "rhetorical drama." In this respect, *The Dismissal* is as Professor Noyes said, a "Renaissance drama such as might have been written anywhere in the Europe of the sixteenth century."[2] As always, Kochanowski's work, though intensely Polish in many ways, can also be placed within a wider, European context.

II   *The Plot*

Very little happens on the stage as the play proceeds; the two Grecian envoys Ulysses and Menelaus come to the palace of

King Priam in Troy to demand the return of their princess
Helen. The Trojans debate at some length what is to be done.
In the end, the Greeks' demand is rejected, and the envoys dismissed. Priam's daughter Cassandra prophesies war and the
subsequent destruction of the city of Troy. The play ends on
this solemn note.

Scholars and others have commented on the various unsatis-
factory aspects of this little drama: it is static, there is no char-
acterization as we understand it in drama, even the "unnatural
language" used by the personages has been criticized. But such
remarks only indicate that the work has been read outside its
historical context, for it is precisely these aspects which make
clear what Kochanowski was doing. Admittedly, there are arguments against reading a literary work inside its historical context, but they do not apply in the Renaissance. Nor should we
forget that Kochanowski was first and foremost a humanist, and
one attribute of a Renaissance humanist was respect for Aristotle,
"the legislator of Parnassus." His play is written to fit Aristotelian
precepts as they were understood in the Polish and Italian
Renaissance, and the play must be regarded in the light of
these precepts.

III Aristotle

The philosophical, rhetorical, and theoretical writings of
Aristotle, who flourished in the fourth century B.C., are an
acquired taste. His ideas seem remote to the general reader and
disputable to critics. But this was not always the case; as late
as the eighteenth century, admirers of Aristotle's writings continued to elevate them to the status of absolute laws in literature, especially poetry and drama—even though Aristotle himself
never laid claim to such authority.

Of Aristotle's writings, the Rhetoric was most highly regarded.
"Rhetoric," as he understood the term, can be briefly described
as "the art of persuading by eloquence," being based on the
study of ancient Greek systems of instruction in various literary
styles and technical devices, intended primarily to exert influence
over an audience.

Rhetoric is the greatest barrier between us and the literature of our ancestors.[3] The study of rhetoric embodied a very old and unbroken European tradition, older than the Church and, indeed, than all Latin literature, for it descends (so we are told) from the Greek Sophists. In the Middle Ages, rhetoric was called the "sweetest of all sciences." Its importance at the University of Padua when Kochanowski was there has already been mentioned. Now, of course, study of rhetoric has been relegated to schools of journalism and less reputable places.

On looking back, however, we can see that the study of rhetoric from ancient times, through the Middle Ages and Renaissance into the eighteenth century, followed a more complex course than the preceding paragraph suggests. Without considering the entire history of the field, we may say that by the fifteenth century (and later), "rhetoric" had replaced poetics and was entirely concerned with what we should now call the "technical" aspects of poetry: meter, rhyme schemes, stanza forms, poetic diction (some words being suitable for poetry, others not), and the like. Much attention was paid to the outward forms of poetry, with stress on the importance of craftsmanship and formal complexity. This interest in technique is no longer fashionable; but in the sixteenth century, when poets were still experimenting in their own languages and had no models from which to work, it was natural.

Poetry as such had by this time become little more than one of the various kinds of rhetoric, having the same function as any other form of discourse—to persuade an audience that something was so, or to persuade an audience that it should act in a given manner. Nowadays, this is the business of a politician rather than a poet. W. A. Auden has said "Poetry makes nothing happen," and John Keats even went so far as to declare "We hate poetry that has a palpable design upon us."

IV The Unities

Among the basic principles which Aristotle laid down for the guidance of playwrights were the unities, including the unity of time, which required that the action of any play take place within three to twenty-four hours. The notion behind this was that a play was more lifelike if the action could be shown to cover a specific period of time. Molière's *Le Misanthrope* was much admired in the seventeenth century, and later, because the action on the stage took exactly as long as it would have done in "real life." Shakespeare's plays were derided in the eighteenth century for failing to observe the unities. The well-made play of the nineteenth century (such as those of Oscar Wilde in the 1890's) adhered strictly to the Aristotelian rule.

The second unity was that of place: again, for many years, the action of a play was confined to one place, often a single room in the house of an important character. Gradually play-wrights ventured to extend the settings of their plays, from one room to another room in the same house, later to the garden of the house. Playwrights made sure that audiences recognized their use of the unities, in a manner which today looks artificial.[4]

Yet another rule attributed to Aristotle required the author of a tragedy to "concentrate on individuals whom the audience can take seriously ... consequently, they must possess some degree of importance." Even Shakespeare observed this dictum, and all classical tragedies are populated by kings and queens, historical or mythological, surrounded by courtiers and set in majestic palaces.

The so-called "unity of action" was also supposed to lend verisimilitude to a play; but Aristotle himself was vague on this rule, and nobody appears to have been able to decide what he meant.

V *Renaissance Drama in Italy*

Aristotle's rhetorical principles were applied to tragedy in Italy as early as 1514, when Trissino composed his celebrated (now forgotten) *Sofonisba*. Although the play was not printed until a decade later, it had gone through six editions by the 1550's, and exercised considerable influence by establishing the tradition of rhetorical drama which flourished in the European theater for almost a century. The tradition was, essentially, that drama was intended to be spoken; action, as we understand it in the theater, was not required.

An influential book in the development of rhetorical drama was Scaliger's *Poetics* (1561), in which the author took the tragedies of Seneca as models. Seneca was a philosopher and playwright (died 65 A.D.) whose tragedies were not meant for public performance. Scaliger's formula for the composition of tragedy, deriving from Seneca, included the introduction of "tragic matters, great and small . . . slayings, despairings, hangings, exiles, bereavements, parricides and incests." Emphasis throughout was placed on long set speeches, ranging from the lyrical to the forensic. The introduction of such characters as messengers or confidantes facilitated or at least gave an excuse for long speeches, which are in effect nothing more than extended monologues.

Senecan tragedy of the kind described here and the rhetorical drama of the Renaissance certainly had features in common; but there were differences, for the tragedies of Seneca and his many imitators took their subjects from classical mythology, whereas the writers of rhetorical drama preferred historical subjects, or at least subjects which passed as historical in those days. Senecan tragedy was little concerned, if at all, with national or political issues of the times: but these were freely introduced into the rhetorical drama.

Professor Weintraub has demonstrated that the *Dismissal of the Grecian Envoys* "does not belong to the dramatic tradition deriving from Seneca," claiming that the tragedy has a "different type of dramatic conflict, another kind of construction of characters, and very different poetic diction."[5] He adds, however, that "Kochanowski was well acquainted with the theater of Seneca which, after all, was the classic tragedy for any educated man of the sixteenth century."

VI *Set Speeches*

The long, indeed often apparently interminable speeches of characters—kings, queens, messengers, and the rest—so characteristic of Seneca's Latin tragedies reappeared in the rhetorical drama practiced in the sixteenth century. The Inns of Court plays, such as Thomas Sackville and Thomas Norton's *Gorboduc* (London, 1561) and other tragedies immediately preceding Shakespeare, are constructed around a series of speeches, and the play was interpreted by contemporary theatergoers as having political significance, warning the English against hostile foreign powers. In France, the *"tragédie oratoire"* has a long tradition, ranging from the playwright Robert Garnier (between 1568 and 1583) to the highly-wrought tragedies of Jean Racine (1639–1699), in which everything depends on the spoken word (in Racine's hands, of course, the word becomes poetry). Other examples of the genre as well as Trissino's *Sofonisba* were written during the Italian Cinquecento.

Tragedy was not the only sixteenth-century genre marked by lengthy set speeches, for they appear in the prose romances, and became a feature of these immense compilations.

Kochanowski's play, while it can conveniently be placed in the genre of rhetorical drama (set speeches, observance of the Aristotelian unities, a subject drawn from "history," and above all the "rhetoric" itself, discussed in the next section), stands out in European literature as the only tragedy of its kind that has remained alive. The play was performed during the Kochanowski four hundredth anniversary proceedings in Cracow in 1935, and recently on Polish television—being well suited to that medium in not requiring elaborate sets or production. The same cannot, of course, be said of the forgotten English Inns of Court tragedies, or the works of any other sixteenth-century practitioners of the genre.

In accordance with the general practice, Kochanowski's dramatic technique is oblique; what we see and hear on the stage during a performance consists of points of rest between action or incidents which the audience never sees. The incidents are described by the characters and again a comparison with Racine's tragedies is unavoidable, though only to a certain limited extent. But both playwrights were interested in the way their characters react to off-stage events, and how they reveal their reactions in speech. Racine's main interest was the states of mind of his characters, whether in the historical tragedies (*Bérénice*), those from Scripture (*Athalie*), or the Greek tragedies (*Andromaque*).

The states of mind reflected in the set speeches cover a wide range, from lyrical meditations to outbursts of rage, from cold argument to doom-laden prophecies. But neither Kochanowski nor his contemporaries thought that drama is something in

which words and action should be interdependent, or that
words and action function together to provide the total dramatic
effect. Shakespeare's genius was, in part, due to the fact that
he divined this, and his plays demonstrate as much.

Providing we accept this limitation in the rhetorical tragedies
of the period, the genre can be seen for what it really was—
the accomplished result of deliberate artistry, or—more often—
craftsmanship. But these qualities are not valued today as they
were in the past, and sometimes what went for craftsmanship
in the sixteenth or eighteenth centuries (the ages in which it
was most highly prized) now seems the height of artifice.

VII   *The Performance*

As we have no record of the first performance of the *Dismissal*, we can only speculate that it took place in the Wawel
palace in front of a decorative wall, such as the facade of a
palace, in this case that of King Priam in Troy. Perhaps there
was an entrance or something more, even a perspective view
of the interior of the building. The text of the play provides
no opportunity for the grandiose scenic effects introduced into
the Baroque theater of the seventeenth century at the court of
King Władysław IV.

The costumes were presumably vaguely Grecian in style,
though (again) the audience would not have been disconcerted
by anachronisms; Antenor says of the prisoner "his costume is
Greek." But we do not know what this meant to a sixteenth-
century audience.

Accounts preserved in the Zamoyski archives include expenses
incurred for the "painting and gilding of scenery," which
suggest that the setting may have been derived from the theater
of Palladio, erected in Venice when Zamoyski was there. Although Kochanowski does not say so, the text of his play indicates that the action occurs throughout in the same place—the
neutral setting so familiar later in eighteenth-century dramaturgy.

VIII   *Set Speeches*

Examples abound in the *Dismissal* of the set speeches which
are characteristic of the rhetorical tragedies from this period.

They range from the elaborate "duel of words" in the first scene between the aged statesman Antenor and Prince Alexander to the highly stylized third chorus imitating a Greek meter, mentioned by Kochanowski in his dedicatory letter. The "duel of words" continues for some sixty lines, as Paris urges Antenor to take his side against the Greeks and they exchange aphorisms, each replying to the key word in the preceding line of his opponent's speech, each reply containing another word which his opponent in turn takes up:

ALEXANDER. As almost all have promised me, I beg
Honored Antenor, that thou too incline
Kindly unto my cause against the Greeks.

ANTENOR. Most eager always am I, noble prince,
To further all that may advance our state,
By making justice triumph in our land.

ALEXANDER. Thou hast no ground to slight a friend's request.

ANTENOR. Nor do I, when he asks a proper thing.

ALEXANDER. To favor more a stranger than a friend,
Methinks is very close akin to envy.

ANTENOR. Seeking to serve one's friend rather than Truth,
Is an offence against all decency.

ALEXANDER. Hand washes hand, the foot supports the foot;
A friend should be a refuge for a friend.

ANTENOR. A mighty friend is Decency; who asks
Service at her expense is no true friend.

(Translated by Ruth Merrill
and George R. Noyes)

ALEKSANDER. Jako mi niemal wszyscy obiecåli,
Cny Antenorze, proszę, i ty sprawie
Mej bądź przychylnym przeciw posłom greckim.

ANTENOR. A ja z chęcią rad, zacny królewicze,
Cokolwiek będzie sprawiedliwość niosła
I dobrze rzeczypospolitej naszej.

ALEKSANDER. Wymówki nie masz gdy przyjaciel prosi.

ANTENOR.   Przyzwalam, kiedy o słuszną rzecz prosi.

ALEKSANDER.   Obcemu więcej życzyć niźli swemu
               Coś niedaleko zda się od zazdrości.

ANTENOR.   Przyjacielowi więcej niźli prawdzie
               Chcieć służyć, zda się przeciw przystojności.

ALEKSANDER.   Ręka umywa rękę, noga nogi
               Wspiera, przyjaciel port przyjacielowi.

ANTENOR.   Wielki przyjaciel przystojności; tą sobie
               Rozkazać służyć nie jest przyjacielska.

                                                   (30–45)

This exchange of dialogue continues for more than twenty lines
in precisely this stilted manner, at the end of which Antenor
refuses to support Alexander in the council that King Priam
has summoned for that very day.

The Chorus makes her first appearance, dividing the drama
into episodes or scenes. Kochanowski has the Chorus speak in
the first person singular, so she is presumably one person rather
than a "chorus." She does not take part in the action, but is no
stranger to what is going on, and may even be present during
the episodes on which she comments. However, her utterances
are at times obscure and some are disputed by scholars to the
present day. Having meditated cryptically on "youth's fire,"
and called on "God in great heaven" (Kochanowski was no more
concerned than Shakespeare with anachronisms), she announces
the entrance of Helen, who "knows the lords / Today decide
her fate; if she must stay in Troy, or revisit Grecian Sparta."

Helen's first speech obeys the rules of rhetorical utterance
as Aristotle recommended, in being a speech of deliberation;
she asks: "What sort of bridal journey will it be, / My home-
coming? Alas! Shall I be dragged / Behind the stern of some
fleet Grecian ship, / A chain around my neck? What countenance / Shall I present in greeting my dear brethren?" She
reveals her attitude toward Alexander by choice of words: he
is "infamous," like a "rapacious wolf" and "an evil man."
Essentially, this speech (twenty-six lines) implies "propositions
relating to possibility and impossibility, and the occurrence or

non-occurrence of events in the past or future" (Aristotle, *Rhetoric* I, 3). Other classes of rhetorical utterance include speeches of exhortation, advice, instigation, discussion, and reprimand; another class includes speeches af accusation, indictment, or defense; a third class encompasses the rhetoric of display—panegyrics, eulogies, funeral orations, speeches honoring or censuring others; and a fourth class includes laments, meditations, vows of vengeance, and other expressions of feeling. All the set speeches in the *Dismissal* can be classified into one or more types, sometimes being a combination.

A scene follows between Helen and an Old Lady, whom Helen addresses as "my mother," but this is clearly figurative. Kochanowski is imitating the conventional "Mistress and Old Nurse" scene in rhetorical tragedy, where the presence of the Old Nurse provides the heroine with the opportunity to expatiate on her plight, while the Nurse gives a speech of advice. In the course of their dialogue, Helen ponders on the nature of "Fortuna," a metaphysical question to which Kochanowski turns time and again in his later work, as will be shown. Helen says:

> But she
> Whose hands control the course of human fate,
> Fortune, all-powerful ruler, witnesseth
> That less prosperity is seen on earth
> Than evil, as men term it. For that queen,
> Though blindly generous, she makes rich a few—
> See with what harsh and grievous poverty
> She tortures all men else . . .
> When she would favor one, she takes the gift,
> Ere she bestows it, from another. . . .

> Ale i ona, która wszytkim włada,
> Która ma wszytko w ręku, wszytkim rządzi,
> Fortuna za mną świadczy, że daleko
> Mniej dóbr na świecie niźli tego, co złym
> Ludzie mianują, bo ubogaciwszy
> Pewna część ludzi, patrzaj, co ich ciężkim
> Ubóstwom trapi.
> . . . i dziś, gdy komu

Chce co uczynić dobrze, pospolicie
Jednemu pierwej weźmie, toż dopiero
Drugiemu daje.

(136–142, 145–148)

When the Chorus reappears, after Helen's scene with the
Old Lady, Kochanowski takes the opportunity to provide her
with a contemporary message, aimed at the illustrious audience.
To be sure, King Stefan Batory knew little or no Polish (he was
Hungarian), but the audience also included important personages; Jan Zamoyski was, for instance, Vice Chancellor of Poland
and later Royal Hetman. The Chorus addresses the audience
directly: "O ye, who rule the republic, / And hold men's justice
in your hands. . . ." The speech emphasizes the responsibility
of Poland's rulers toward those they govern, for the tasks, duties,
and responsibilities of princes were a matter of great concern
to thinking men of the Renaissance and appropriate for mention in a rhetorical drama. Castiglione's courtiers discussed
them, as did the Polish courtiers in Górnicki's paraphrase. Familiar echoes occur in *King Lear* and *Hamlet,* and the theme is
one which Kochanowski had broached ten years earlier in *The
Satyr* and *Concord.*
The gravity of the matter is stressed in the final lines: "For
we can see, / The crimes of those in high authority / Have
ruined fairest cities, to the ground / Have overthrown wide
empires. . . ."

IX *The Messenger*

Helen enters again: she is joined by a Messenger (Poseł),
who announces "good news" to his mistress. She commands him
to relate what has occurred during the Trojan council. His reply
forms the central section of the play, being one hundred and
fifty lines in length or almost one fourth of the whole. Indeed,
the Messenger's speech is longer than any monologue in the
classical Greek tragedies and even in Senecan drama.
In accordance with the rules, Kochanowski describes the
crucial meeting of the Trojans, rather than depicting it on the
stage. The Messenger begins at the beginning: "First spake the

King, when all our lords were set / In council." Alexander speaks next, defending his abduction of Helen: "Venus gave her to me, / And I accepted gratefully." He reminds the Trojans that the Greeks "stole Medea from the house of our friends, / And was it not fitting that I repay / Their stratagem with an identical stratagem? / If I am guilty, then so are they." King Priam has suffered injustices at the hands of the Greeks also: "Even now / Still lie the ruined walls upon the ground; / The fields today, marks of the Grecian sword, / Of his cruel hand, are spread out desolate." (The reference is to Greek mythology: Priam's father, King Laomedon, had promised the hand of his daughter Hesione to the Greek hero Heracles, if the latter would rid Troy of a sea monster, Heracles slew the monster, but Laomedon refused to keep the promise, whereupon Heracles slew him and gave Hesione as a slave to one of his comrades.) Alexander points out that "if Hesione / is still alive / She is living in Greek captivity."

Antenor, the elder statesman, speaks next; he remains hostile to Alexander, as he was during the play's exposition, and declares that when Alexander abducted Helen, he was a guest of the Greeks: "Forgetful of the laws that bind a guest, / He seized his host's wife and made her his own." Antenor insists that Helen be returned to the Greeks, as the envoys demand, for law and decorum demand it. He also warns the assembled councillors that, were Alexander to marry Helen, the downfall of the city of Troy would follow, and all would have to pay with their own blood.

The Messenger enumerates the opinions of other members of the council; the last was a certain Iketaon, who urged that the Trojans declare war on the Greeks, for their greed "never stays within bounds; / like a flood / It imperceptibly overflows its boundaries, / Until it covers all the fields." Iketaon's speech is one of persuasion, and it succeeds in swaying the councillors: a few dissident voices (says the Messenger) were shouted down, and the council issued an order that "Helen remain in Troy, until the Greeks compensate us for Medea." Finally, the Messenger urges Helen to join Alexander, and both leave the stage.

The Chorus comments briefly on the defeat of the Greek envoys, whom she now sees approaching "hanging their heads."

This is a somewhat primitive, though acceptable, way of introducing new characters to the audience. They are Ulysses and Menelaus; the former delivers a speech of indictment (lines 383–409). Troy, he declares, is "a kingdom of anarchy, close to destruction, / Where laws count for nothing, and justice / has no place. Everything must be purchased for gold." Menelaus then utters a vow of vengeance (lines 410–424), calling upon "the eternal light of heaven and you, O fertile earth, / And thou, spacious ocean, all you gods, / Both high and low, bear witness this day to me." The Trojans in council had met his plea for justice with mockery, and he longs to "feed his sword with blood."

X *The Third Chorus*

Kochanowski uses the last appearance of the Chorus for a metrical experiment, to which he had referred in the dedicatory letter to Zamoyski. Instead of the regular thirteen-syllabic blank verse which all the other characters speak, the Chorus on this occasion delivers an extended invocation to the "beech boat" made from trees felled on Mount Ida, which had brought Alexander to Greece for the abduction of Helen. The metrical pattern depends on stress and, to a lesser degree, on the length of certain vowels, imitated from the Greek and impossible to render in English with the same stylistic effects:

> O white-winged sailer of the sea,
>> Reared upon Ida's lofty steep,
>> Vessel of beech which o'er the deep
> With its wet salt paths bore buoyantly
>> The fair-faced shepherd, Priam's son,
>> To the Eurotas' crystal flood.

> O białoskrzydła morska pławaczko,
> Wychowanico Idy wysokiej,
> Łodzi bukowa, któraś gładkiej
> Twarzy pasterza Pryjamczyka
> Mokrymi słonych wód ścieżkami
> Do przezroczystych Eurotowych
> Brodów nosiła!

(425–430)

This metrical experiment was to remain unique in Polish poetry until the twentieth century, when Jan Kasprowicz attempted similar experiments.

As we have seen, some of Kochanowski's contemporaries also made similar experiments, including Edmund Spenser, Sir Philip Sidney, and John Donne (somewhat later). But, as in the case of Kochanowski, their experiments led nowhere; they all failed to realize that prosody in any language is based on phonetic facts, not arbitrary rules as to the length of vowels. Neither Polish nor English had such "rules," and no attempts to invent them could succeed. In France, Ronsard tried similar experiments, imitating the Greek method of singing poetry to a musical instrument, or at least accommodating French poetry to music. In Italy, Claudio Tolomei (1492–1555) tried to enrich the vernacular metrical system by forms based on quantity. All these poets, including Kochanowski, evidently believed that since Latin poetry had derived its prosody from Greek, then the vernaculars could obtain theirs from the Latin.

Perhaps Kochanowski wanted the third chorus to be chanted, or sung to a musical accompaniment. But as there is no record or account of the 1578 performance, this must remain a hypothesis. In any case, the strict pattern forced Kochanowski to adopt involved syntax, e.g., "by wet paths of salt water" (mokrymi słonych wód ścieżkami), "Venus most beautiful of all the goddesses" (ze wszech Wenus Bogiń piękniejsza), and "beneath the walls / Enemy trenches will stand" (a pod mury / Nieprzyjacielskie staną szańce). The last example, where an epithet is separated by a verb, or other word, from the noun it qualifies became a favorite device of prosody in the eighteenth century; the arrangement cannot, of course, be used in English, but in Polish the word order is considerably less rigid.

XI *Cassandra*

The third speech of the Chorus holds overtones of prophecy, when "huge trumpets will sound, and beneath the walls of Troy / Enemy trenches will stand." The prophecy is taken up by King Priam and Antenor, who now enter; the latter warns the king that war between the Trojans and Greeks is certain, as a result of the dismissal of the Grecian envoys by the king's council. News is already reaching Troy of the Grecian army assembling. The Trojans must "either fight / or flee; there is no third choice."

Their dialogue is interrupted as Antenor catches sight of a woman "with hair disordered and a pale countenance, / Her limbs trembling, her bosom heaving, She rolls her eyes, shakes her head; now she would speak, / Now falls silent." Priam informs Antenor (for the benefit of the audience) that she is his "unhappy daughter Cassandra," who has been seized by the Apollonian spirit of prophecy. According to mythology, Apollo, the god of prophecy, had fallen in love with Cassandra and bestowed his gift of prophecy upon her. But Cassandra spurned the god and, in anger, he decreed that no one should believe her prophecies, thus rendering his gift useless.

Cassandra advances, lamenting that her utterances "all go to the wind, having no more credulence among men / Than vain tales and waking dreams." Nevertheless, she prophesies: first she sees "a hind, swimming in deep sea." This is an animal of evil omen, and she implores the Trojans not to let it come on shore, for it will bring "downfall, conflagration, desolation." Next, she sees Greek horsemen threatening the walls of Troy, and the corpse of her brother Alexander. The third section of Cassandra's vision is devoted to the wooden horse which the Greeks were to use to enter the walls of Troy; she urges the Trojans to burn the horse "lest you yourselves be burned by it." The catalogue of disasters continues, until the Chorus intervenes to lead away the "suffering maiden." Cassandra's prophetic lament is peculiar to the Troy legend, and is found in other versions, including Lydgate's *Troy Book*.

Since the action of the play was restricted by the Aristotelian rules to a single day, Kochanowski could not show the true catastrophe, or climax, of the events he dramatizes (the destruction of the city of Troy). Thus he uses Cassandra's prophecy to serve this purpose. It is an ingenious solution to a difficult technical problem.

After the Chorus has led the distracted Cassandra away, Antenor begs Priam to heed her words and not take them as vain; and the king admits they alarmed him, particularly in view of a dream in which his late wife appeared to him, and she "instead of a child" (Alexander) "gave birth to a fire-brand."

The last scene begins with the entrance of a Trojan officer bringing in a prisoner in Greek costume. The latter has informed his captors that "a thousand galleys are in readiness / At Aulida, only awaiting the envoys' return." At this news, Priam announces that he will immediately summon a council of defense for Troy; but Antenor suggests the council should be one of war, not delay.

XII *Political Aspects*

Kochanowski's continued preoccupation with the security of Poland and his fears of her unreadiness in case of attack were described already in his earliest poems: the situation of the Trojans and Greeks in the *Dismissal of the Grecian Envoys* seems to reflect that of the Poles and the Muscovites. Indeed, the play was staged "in a climate of acute political excitement."[6] Ivan the Terrible had decided to invade the tributary duchy of Livonia (northeast of Poland) and the Poles were preparing for war.

So Kochanowski emphasized his political views in a Latin poem, "Orpheus Sarmaticus," which was recited after the performance of the *Dismissal,* and which the king would understand:

> Poles, what hopes and designs do you nourish
>   in your hearts?
> This is no time for idleness, sleep: nor for
>   festivities with a lute, cup or light dances.
> From the east, the rider hurls his venomed arrows,
>   as dangerous in attack as in retreat.
> He leads his troops from the hyperborean fields.
> He is hardened in Ural snows, and the frost of
>   his country.
> And if I am to tell the truth, his glory is due
>   only to your sloth.
> He has allies who, using false words, enter into
>   alliance with you, but in their hearts
>   conceal thoughts of war.
> Envy and deceived hopes torture their spirits.

The reference here may be to Austria; next, Kochanowski describes the Turkish threat:

Why should I mention the conqueror of Asia and
    tyrant of Europe?
Our ancestors feared him, even when he sailed
    through the distant Ionian Sea
In a thousand ships, and besieged the Island of
    Rhodes.
Now that victor of land and on sea dominates the
    entire Danube with his fleet,
And spreading terror, rules over both its banks.
    Not content,
He has led his troops to the Dniester and looks
    with greedy eyes
At the fields of Podolia.

                    (Translated by Czesław Miłosz)

After a rousing call to arms echoing that of Antenor at the
end of the *Dismissal*, Kochanowski ends the poem with praise
for King Stefan Batory, a man "not given to drinking, dancing
and merrymaking, but trained for military action."[7]

But Poland was also suffering from internal strife, and this
state of affairs may be reflected in the dissension within the
Trojan council, as reported to Helen by the Messenger. Members of the Sejm (Chamber of Deputies) were suspicious of
the foreign king Batory, and, indeed, an openly hostile faction
was deliberately harassing his preparations for a large-scale
invasion of Muscovy. Fortunately, Batory proved equal to the
occasion, made a formal declaration of war against Muscovy in
1579, and captured the key city of Polotsk, thus regaining an
entire province that had been lost to Poland during the reign
of King Zygmunt August fifteen years before.

A few anachronisms were probably intended to point in the
direction Kochanowski's audience was to look: King Piram himself cannot reach a decision of his own, but must summon and
consult his council—a situation that reflects the inability of the
Polish king to initiate action without the approval of the Chamber of Deputies. The noisy, even unruly dispute of the Trojan
council, as described by the Messenger, resembles the often
disorderly proceedings in the Chamber, a state of affairs which
prevailed in that gathering until the Partitions brought the proceedings to an end. License to brawl, shout down, and veto

opponents in the Chamber was prized by the Polish gentry as their much-boasted "golden freedom," but this inability to reach agreement among themselves and the hostility toward reforms of any kind on the part of certain Deputies gravely weakened the State apparatus. Kochanowski and other farseeing patriots knew, as early as the sixteenth century, how disastrous the effects of this state of affairs would be.

XIV   Style, Diction, Versification

Professor Weintraub holds that Kochanowski composed the *Dismissal* in unrhymed or blank verse because he took the system over from Trissino's *Sofonisba*. This may well be so, but the Latin and Greek dramatists did not use rhyme either, and as John Milton pointed out a century later rhyme in tragic poetry was never a "necessary adjunct or true ornament of poetry or good verse, in longer works especially." Any poet brought up on the classical writers would have concurred with Milton that rhyme "is the invention of a barbarous age, to set off wretched matter and lame meter," adding

not without cause therefore, both Italian and Spanish poets of prime note have rejected rhyme . . . as have also long since our best English tragedies. This neglect of rhyme is so little to be taken for a defect, though it may seem so perhaps to vulgar readers, that it is rather to be esteemed an example of ancient liberty restored.

(*Paradise Lost*, preface, 1668)

Kochanowski's poetic diction in the *Dismissal* is characteristic of his style at its most elevated, as befits his elevated characters; he avoids Seneca's hyperbole, the startling contrasts and lists of horrors so admired by other sixteenth-century playwrights, including the young Shakespeare (*Timon of Athens*). The lines follow smoothly, with frequent enjambements (considerably more than in the *Psalms*, for instance). Again this smoothness is appropriate for what is, after all, *speech.*

Although stylized language is used by all the characters, each is to some degree individualized; Priam is mindful of his royal rank, Antenor is the tactful rather pompous statesman (Polonius in *Hamlet* comes to mind), Alexander is hot-tempered. Cas-

sandra's monologue prophesying disaster differs somewhat from
the speeches of the others: she is in a state of inspiration, utter-
ing rhetorical questions and exclamations:

> Why vainly dost thou torture me, Apollo,
> Who, when thou lent'st me power of prophecy,
> Gav'st to my words no weight, but unto the winds
> Fly all my prophecies, gaining with men
> Credence accorded dreams and idle tales?
> My fettered heart, my loss of memory,
> Whom will they aid? To whom is profitable
> This alien spirit, speaking through my lips,
> And all my thoughts, ruled over by a guest
> Grievous, unbearable?

> Po co mię prózno, srogi Apollo, trapisz,
> Który, wieszczego ducha dawszy, nie daleś
> Wagi w słowiech, ale me wszytki proroctwa
> Na wiatr idą, nie mając u ludzi więcej
> Wiary nad baśni prózne i sny znikome?
> Komu serce spętane albo pamięci
> Zguba moja pomoże? Komu z ust moich
> Duch nie mój pożyteczen i zmysły wszytki,
> Ciężkim, nieznośnym gościem opanowane?
>
> (500–508)

One question remains: why did Kochanowski's *Dismissal of
the Grecian Envoys* remain unique in Polish literature for over
two hundred years? The theater and dramaturgy were strangely
late in reaching Poland, and indeed there was no national
theater until the Age of Enlightenment (1764). To be sure,
wealthy magnates occasionally staged plays in private, as did
their contemporaries in Russia, but no theatrical tradition
emerged. Professor Claude Backvis sees the *Dismissal* as "a proto-
type of the future of Polish theater"[8] and supports his view with
ingenious arguments. But the fact remains that Kochanowski
was by nature a lyric poet, not a dramatist.

CHAPTER 6

Joys and Sorrows of Life (The Epigrams)

THROUGHOUT his life Kochanowski wrote epigrams in Polish as well as in Latin; however, the Polish epigrams were not collected and printed until 1584, the year of the poet's death. But they circulated in manuscript copies and were known to his contemporaries. The epigrams range from lyrical poems to anecdotes in versified form, and when printed became one of the poet's most popular books, being reprinted twelve times in the next fifty years.

He called them "fraszki" (trifles), thus seeming to flaunt Martial's statement that "anyone who calls epigrams mere frivolous trifles does not understand what they are" (IV, lix). But, as we shall see, Kochanowski's collection of "trifles" brings us closer to him as an individual than any of his other poetry, even the *Laments*.

Other Polish writers before him had written epigrams, including Mikołaj Rej, who published a number of what he called "figliki." This set of eight-line epigrams keeps to a strict metrical pattern which soon becomes monotonous—a characteristic of Rej's verse. Structurally, they are close to the "emblem," a minor poetic genre invented in the 1520's by the Italian poet Alciati.[1] The emblem consists of a woodcut, usually allegorical, with a motto to suit, and a short poem expounding the significance of the woodcut. Thus Rej's first four lines will present an allegory, with the remaining four commenting upon it. Although Rej's are somewhat limited (as all emblems were), they widened the thematic range of the epigram in Polish, for Rej included versified "portraits" of contemporaries, anecdotes from court and everyday life, occasional verses, and satire.

As a more conscious literary artist than Rej, Kochanowski made his epigrams a great deal more varied in both content and metrical pattern. Here he displays the classical love of *varietas* which Latin poets strove for in their collections, and he declares that "here frivolous epigrams are mixed with serious [ones]" (III, 39). Unfortunately, the order in which Kochanowski wrote the epigrams (there are 295 altogether) is not established; nor do we know whether their arrangement in three books was that of the poet, or his printer.[2]

The epigrams vary in length from two to twenty lines, but the standard is the four-line stanza which derives, of course, from Horace. We take the four-line stanza in all European poetry for granted; but for Kochanowski the debt was surely there.

I *Autobiography*

Interested persons have for many years subjected Kochanowski's epigrams (and his other poetry as well) to close scrutiny, in the hope of unearthing biographical details. Miłosz calls the collection "a sort of very personal diary, but one where the personality of the author never appears in the foreground."[3] This approach, however, merely produces unreliable speculation, even fallacies and mistakes. W. H. Auden's comments on the identity of the "dark lady" of Shakespeare's sonnets are relevant here.[4] In any event, Kochanowski himself warns us not to attempt this approach, declaring he had placed all his secrets in them, but that it is "fruitless" for anybody to trouble his brain since he will "wander into a strange labyrinth" (III, 29).

All the same, Kochanowski's epigrams are "personal," in that they consist of his own individual, personal observations: they are not generalizations capable of *universal* application. They can properly be read as expressions of the poet's personality— which is something different from autobiographical facts. To judge from the collection, Kochanowski was much concerned (like everybody else) with such matters as family life on his country estate at Czarnolas, with love, friendship, nature, music and song, conviviality, the pleasures and pathos of ordinary life —none of which differed materially from ordinary life in the present day. As befits the genre, which was considered "low," we also find sketches of social life and manners of the times, satire (against corrupt clergy, for instance), epitaphs, comments on human vices (against drunkenness), philosophical reflections, epigrams composed for special occasions, even celebrating heroes of antiquity. But the last are not treated seriously:

> My verses care not
> For important heroes.
> Mars, though warlike,
> And fleet-footed Apollo are absent;
> But laughter and jokes
> My pages are wont to gather.
>
> (I, 2)

> Nie dbają moje papiery
> O przeważne bohatery;
> Nie u nich Mars, chocia srogi,
> I Achilles prędkonogi;
> Ale śmiechy, ale żarty
> Zwykły zbierać moje karty.

II *Love*

Among various ladies to whom Kochanowski addresses epigrams are Lidia, Anna, Reina, Magdalena, Zofia, Jadwiga, and Hanna. Scholarly ingenuity has been exercised on the identities of these ladies, but to little effect. We do not even know whether all or, indeed, any of them existed. Kochanowski's wife was named Dorota.

Four of the epigrams are addressed simply "To a Girl" (Do dziewki), demonstrating Kochanowski's ability to deal with the same topic in different tones of voice. The first (II, 33) is rhetorical; the poet uses language to persuade the girl to bestow her favors upon him before it is too late. He declares:

> Now you can surround your beautiful hair with lilies,
> Now you can sing and dance;
> After a while another girl will come, whom you exceed in years,
> And say: "You take the distaff; I am more suited to courtship."

> Teraz możesz lelią piękny włos otoczyć,
> Teraz możesz zaśpiewać, możesz w tańcy skoczyć;

Po chwili przydzie druga, którą przejdziesz laty,
I rzeczeć: "Weźm ty kądziel; przystojniej mnie w swaty."

The *carpe diem* theme ("make hay while the sun shines") is
one to which Kochanowski never tired of reverting.

In the second epigram (II, 72), Kochanowski elaborates a
conventional idea: he is "troubled by everlasting longing; / As
though the sun had gone in, when you are not here, / But with
you half a night seems a day in heaven." In the third (III, 13),
the girl is accused of cruelty (a common accusation in Petrarchan
poetry), and the eighteen-line poem ends with a somewhat
cynical remark:

> Love has its ways,
> It knows that which is better, yet prefers the worse.
> And you, if you would quench my hope of your favors,
> Have long since been desiring my death.

> . . . Miłość ma swe obyczaje,
> Zna, co lepiej, a przedsię przy gorszym zostaje.
> A ty, jeśli nadzieję chcesz o łasce swojej
> Zgasić we mnie, już dawno pragniesz śmierci mojej.

The last of this group (III, 82) is a Polish version of an Anacreontic epigram, "Do not flee from me, delightful maiden." This
may be one of the later epigrams of the collection, since the
poet refers to his "gray beard" while assuring the girl that his
"heart is not yet old" and that "Garlic has a white head, but its
tail is green."

A handful of the epigrams are directed against *old* women, and
here again Kochanowski is looking back to classical models,[5]
when poets satirized women trying to conceal their age under
a coat of paint. Martial, for instance, declared: "Polla, you try
to cover up your wrinkles with powder and paint, / But you're
only fooling yourself" (III, xlii), and went even further in the
epigram beginning "Thaïs stinks . . ." (VI, xciii). Such scorn for
old age in women was widely current among humanistic writers
of the Renaissance, who may have gone back to the medieval
belief that women were tools of the Devil. A reaction against
the Petrarchan cult of woman perhaps contributed also. Kochanowski says:

Now you would like to flirt with me,
When you have grown old, poor woman.
Let me alone, for God's sake! You can surely see
That the thorn is useless, when the rose has faded.

(I, 7)

Teraz by ze mną zygrywać się chciała,
Kiedyś, niebogo, sobie podstarzała.
Daj pokój, prze Bóg! Sama baczysz snadnie,
Że nie po cierniu, kiedy róża spadnie.

A couplet entitled "The Sacrifice" reads: "Lais has sacrificed her mirror to Pafija. / She does not wish to see what she is; she cannot see what she used to be" (II, 30). (Pafijej swe źwierciadło Lais poświęciła. / Nie chce się widzieć, czym jest; nie moze, czym była.) The gallery also includes an "Epitaph to a Drunken Old Woman" (II, 70) cast entirely in the form of a dialogue between the poet and the tomb itself, which answers for the old woman.

III   *Friendship*

During Kochanowski's stay at various royal and other courts, he gained the friendship and patronage of a number of aristocrats, Polish and foreign. They included Mikołaj Mielecki, Starosta of Chelm, later Palatine and Hetman, to whom the poet offers "a few verses" on the occasion of Mielecki's setting out on a journey (I, 45); Mikołej Firlej, Palatine of Cracow, to whom two epigrams are inscribed (I, 26 and III, 73); Stanisław Wapowski, courtier and diplomatist (III, 24); Wacław Ostroróg, protector of the Czech Brotherhood in Poland (III, 64); Jadam Konarski, scholar and diplomatist (III, 69); Mikołaj Wolski, another scholar, whose collection of Spanish books is preserved in the library of the Jagellonian University (III, 77); and Andrzej Trzecieski, who wrote Latin poetry, translated some Psalms, and supported the Reformation in Poland (II, 80). Foreigners to whom Kochanowski dedicated one or more epigrams included Dr. Jacob Montanus, the philosopher who later became an Archdeacon of Lublin (II, 35 and others); and Pedro Ruiz de Moros, professor of law at Cracow between 1541 and 1550, later courtier and legal adviser to King Zygmunt August.[6] Kochanowski asks his noble friends to "remember him," or thanks them for their hospitality; but his tone is never servile.

Not all Kochanowski's friends were aristocrats or scholars with names still remembered in history. As he says: "What is life without friends? A prison. / No one to help, no one to mourn you, / None to rejoice with you" (II, 48). When he claims that he chooses friends for their "virtue and sense" (II, 55), we can believe him. Noble birth or "villages full of serfs, or money" (II, 99) are no criteria. Friendship, after all, is a "powerful knot, more lasting than others, / Which the daughters of beautiful memory (the Muses) have tied" (II, 104). Friends are especially to be cherished in times of "sore distress," when the heart is "devoured by unsleeping cares" (II, 61).

On the other hand, Kochanowski can also laugh at his friends, even making epigrams on their physical defects, this being an age when such blemishes as a big nose or ears or baldness were treated more coarsely than at present. Addressing a certain "little Pawel," Kochanowski warns him:

> When the cranes fly in from the sea,
> Do not, O Pawel, frequent the outdoors,
> Lest they peck your skin,
> In the belief you are a Pygmy.
>
> > (I, 48)

> Kiedy żorawie polecą za morze,
> Nie bywaj często, Pawełku, na dworze,
> Aby na tobie nie poklwali skóry,
> Mnimając, żeś ty z Pigmeolów który.

(The reference is to the account in the *Iliad* of a battle between cranes and a Pygmy tribe.)

A certain Slasa evidently possessed a large nose: Kochanowski urges him to "stand facing the sun, / Open wide your mouth, Mr. Slasa, / And we shall need no other sundial; / For that nose which sticks out, / Will show on your teeth, what time it is" (I, 95). Another friend by the name of Bartosz is teased:

O bald Bartosz, with your Spanish-style beard,
You are worthy of favors for your charms;
But young ladies are unkind to you,
They say you're a great ne'er-do-well;
If this is so, your charm
And the bald patch, and the beard, are all in vain.

(II, 45)

Bartoszu łysy, a z hiszpańską brodą,
Godzien by łaski za swoją urodą;
Ale panienki na cię niełaskawy,
Tak powiadają, żeś nogieć wąchawy;
Co jeśli tak jest, szkodać i urody,
I tej łysiny, i tej czystej brody.

Some of the "jokes" which Kochanowski uses as a basis for epigrams are very ancient indeed; one brief anecdote, "On Chmura," describes Mr. Chmura's cook serving him on a cloudy day a roast crow instead of a capon (I, 97), the "point" being that Chmura also signifies "cloud."

Even marital infidelity comes in for its share of mockery in "To a Mathematician":

He discovered the age of the sun, and he knows
Just why the wrong or the right wind blows.
He has looked at each nook of the ocean's floor,
But he doesn't see that his wife is a whore.

(Peterkiewicz and Singer; I, 53)

Ziemię pomierzył i głębokie morze,
Wie, jako wstają i zachodzą zorze;
Wiatrom rozumie, praktykuje komu,
A sam nie widzi, że ma kurwę w domu.

Sometimes the poet's tone is peevish, as when he explains to Piotr why he avoids him: "I cannot listen any longer to your stupid chatter" (II, 17), and Wojtek fares no better: "You ask me whether I am not bored, sitting by myself? / I am more bored with you, O Wojtek, since you inquire" (II, 36). Marcin is told that although the epigrammatist believes in the "music

of the spheres" of which philosophers speak, he cannot tolerate
Marcin's music-making (II, 59).

Friendship is associated with wine and conviviality, as it has
been since Horace. In the epigram to a Spanish doctor (I, 79),
Kochanowski again uses dialogue to make his point:

"Our good doctor would leave us and go to bed,
Nor does he want to spend the evening with us."
"Let him alone! We'll find him in bed,
And in the meantime, let's be merry!"
"Supper is over now, let's go to the Spaniard's."
"Yes, let's be off, but not without a flask of wine."
"Let us in, dear doctor, agreeable companion!"
The doctor would not let them in, but the door did.
"One drink won't do any harm, may God preserve you!"
"Providing it's only one," said the doctor to this.
From one it passed to nine.
The doctor's brain was in a whirl.
"Oh dear," says he, "how to keep up with these gentlemen?
I go to bed sober, but get up tipsy."

"Nasz dobry doktór spać się od nas bierze,
Ani chce z nami doczekać wieczerze."
"Dajcie mu pokój! najdziem go w pościeli,
A sami przedsię bywajmy weseli!"
"Już po wieczerzy, pódźmy do Hiszpana!"
"Ba, wierę, pódźmy, ale nie bez dzbana."
"Puszczaj, doktorze, towarzyszu miły!"
Doktór nie puścił, ale drzwi puściły.
Jedna nie wadzi, daj ci Boże zdrowie!"
"By jeno jedna"—doktór na to powie.
Od jednej przyszło aż więc do dziewiąci,
A doktorowi mózg się we łbie mąci.
"Trudny"—powiada, "mój rząd z tymi pany:
Szedłem spać trzeźwio, a wstanę pijany."

This unedifying, slightly disreputable incident is remarkable
for the economy of means by which Kochanowski obtains his
effect. The characters are not even named, nor described; what
they say is sufficient. Their reasons for making the doctor "go
to bed sober, but get up tipsy" are not explained, and time is

telescoped between lines six and seven, during which the tipplers proceed from supper to the house of their victim.

Another epigram dealing with a doctor is entirely different in tone:

> Anyone may boldly call you an arch-doctor,
> For you know not only how to cure physical illness,
> But you also know many stratagems to produce
> a cheerful mind:
> Wine, a lute, a girl—to cheer me up.
>
> (II, 87)

> Arcydoktorem cię zwać każdy może śmiele,
> Bo ty nie tylko umiesz zleczeć niemoc w ciele,
> Ale i na dorbrą myśl masz fortelów wiele:
> Wino, lutnią, podwikę; to mi to wesele.

Wine reappears in other epigrams. Kochanowski declares: "I never cared for gold, / All I asked for / Was a tankard before me, / And a friend drinking with me . . ." (III, 4), and admits: "I write just as I live; / My poems are tipsy, for I am glad to drink" (III, 17). He confesses to a friend: "Denial is vain, I got drunk; / With wine? Or with poetry? / If with wine, then its fumes were subtle . . ." (III, 64). He also felt inspired to write the Anacreontic "In Defense of Drunkards":

> Earth, that drinks rain, refreshes the trees;
> Oceans drink rivers; stars quaff up the seas;
> So why should they make such a terrible fuss
> Over insignificant tipplers like us?
> (Peterkiewicz and Singer; I, 57)

> Ziemia deszcz pije, ziemię drzewa piją,
> Z rzek morze, z morza wszytki gwiazdy zyją.
> Na nas nie wiem, co ludzie upatrzyli,
> Dziwno im, żeśmy trochę się napili.

Another version of this epigram was written by Adam Naruszewicz, the earliest poet of the Polish Age of Enlightenment and contemporary of Ignacy Krasicki. The verse was first printed in the 1770's in Naruszewicz's *Anakreona pieśni wybrane* (Selected Songs of Anacreon, no. XIII).

> The barren earth drinks rain,
> The tree lives by earthy juice,
> The air grazes on sea,
> The sun washes in the sea:
> The moon swallows a bright gleam
> From the sun's ray:
> But you gaze upon me,
> Wishing me not to drink wine?

> Płonna ziemia deszcze pije,
> Drzewo ziemnym sokiem żyje,
> Powietrze się morzem pasie,
> Słońce w morzu omywa się;
> Od słonecznego promyka
> Księżyc jasny blask połyka:
> A tyś na mnie oczy wlepił,
> Chcąc, ażebym wina nie pił?

Although Naruszewicz was in many ways of interest as a literary figure (occupying much the same place in Polish literature as Dryden in English), his version—with its conventional epithets, making it twice the length of Kochanowski's—demonstrates Naruszewicz's lack of artistry when compared with that of Kochanowski.

These vinous epigrams reveal an aspect of the poet's personality very different from the politically-minded writer of the *Dismissal of the Grecian Envoys* or the elevated stylist of the *Psalms*.

IV *Family Life*

Kochanowski's years of retired country life on his estate at Czarnolas constituted his most productive period. In "To the Mountains and Forests" (III, 1), he expresses his joy at the landscape of "High mountains and leafy forests," then looks back at his own life, his years of travel "across deep seas," visiting France, Germany, Italy, and the "Sybilline grottoes," as a student, a knight, a courtier in a "lordly palace." He compares himself to Proteus, "Changing now into a dragon, / Now into rain, into fire, into a rainbow." Finally, he wonders, "What will be next?"—little knowing that he would soon marry the "inestimable Dorota" and become the father of a family.

Kochanowski was fond of a linden tree in his Czarnolas garden, and wrote three epigrams on it. The best-known is an invitation to a guest to seat himself "under my leaves, and repose! / The sun does not penetrate here, I promise you." Cool winds blow from the fields, nightingales sing, bees collect honey, and the linden tree knows how to lull guests to sleep with its "quiet whisper" (II, 6). In a later epigram, the tree again invites a "learned guest" to take shelter from the heat, with a "lute and jug of cool wine from the well" (III, 6).

An eight-line epigram "On My House at Czarnolas" is a prayer of thanksgiving, asking God to bless the home which Kochanowski values above "marble palaces with gilded walls," and he asks for "health and a clean conscience, / Wholesome food, the benevolence of others, / Good manners and a tolerable old age" (III, 37).

V *Philosopher*

Kochanowski's vocation was that of a poet, not a philosopher, theologian, preacher, or anything else; so we do not find, or expect, profound philosophical utterances in his poetry. But as an individual of high intellectual attainments and great sensitivity, he was certainly interested in matters pertaining to philosophy—life, death, the vanity of this world, Fortuna and her mysterious ways—ideas that he could apply both to his own life and that of his fellowmen. Indeed, two epigrams are entitled "On Human Life," and in them Kochanowski speculates on mysteries that have been the preoccupation of poets from time immemorial: "Everything we think is but a trifle, / Everything we do is but a trifle, / In this world nothing is certain," and the poet reminds us that "Honor, beauty, power, money, fame, / All pass away like leaves of grass" (I, 3). In the last epigram of Book One, Kochanowski sees human life as children at play, watched by "Everlasting Thought" (a humanistic way of referring to God) and ending in misfortune or death (I, 101).

Man as "God's plaything" derives, of course, from classical Greek, and Kochanowski elaborates on the theme again in an epigram with that title (III, 76): "When did man ever behave so wisely, / That God did not have to laugh at him?" Indeed, "Man, blinded by self-love, / Believes that the world was created for his benefit"—an echo of pre-Copernican theory (see chapter 1).

General truths of which many poets felt it their duty to remind readers include epigrams that declare: "True wealth depends on the mind; / Silver, gold and money are secondary" (I, 46), and "If you are to die, what use is gold? I wish always to enjoy good thoughts, / And pass time with friends" (I, 76).

Death is a constant theme; over twenty of the epigrams are epitaphs for various people, and also animals (a horse, III, 75, and a cat, III, 52). Like Latin epitaphs, these take various forms: sometimes the poet is speaking, sometimes the dead person speaks or the epitaph is a dialogue ("On a Drunken Old Lady," already mentioned). Some are straightforward panegyrics: "Old people mourn you, young people too, / The court is all in mourning for you, Kryski..." (I, 64), or teach a moral lesson, as in an epitaph on a tavern keeper murdered by "ruffians," which ends with the poet entreating passersby to "curse drunkenness" (I, 71). The death of children is mourned, with the child speaking to the father, urging him not to weep because "my innocence has raised me to Heaven" (I, 81)—foreshadowing Kochanowski's later *Laments* on the death of his small daughter, Ursula. Elsewhere the father speaks: "I was a father, today I have no one / To call me that... Death has devoured my all" (I, 93).

That Death comes to all men is a truism, but Kochanowski does not hesitate to remind us of that too. In the "Epitaph to Doctor Adrian" (II, 75), he bids farewell to Adrian and points out that "Herbs are no help, / He whom Death takes, must resign himself." At times, Kochanowski's epitaphs on now-forgotten friends and boon companions strike a note of genuine feeling, as when he addresses a certain Kos: "My good Kos, your companions / Have placed your dead corpse in this tomb, / Who were merry with you yesterday. / Death comes for man at all times" (I, 31), and "Yesterday he drank with us, but today we bury him... / Death knows neither gold nor costly purple, / It pounces as on a hen in a hen-coop" (I, 32). The rustic imagery here, while bordering on the grotesque, nevertheless reflects Kochanowski's attitude as a countryman, to whom the loss of a hen to a fox or other predatory animal may well give rise to thoughts barely comprehensible to a more sophisticated town dweller.

Epigrams on youth and old age respectively follow each other (I, 82–83): "They might expect to have a year without Spring, / Who wish that the young did not riot," and "Poor old age, we all crave you, / But when you come, we complain." As elsewhere in his work, Kochanowski here is not stating anything original, but—as in all his writings—the generalizations are true and have the weight of universal human experience behind them.

A central philosophical or even metaphysical question with which Kochanowski was increasingly concerned throughout his life was how much man's life is influenced by Fortuna, who can also be called Destiny, or Fate, or Providence, or Chance.[7] The theme is, of course, linked with that of man as God's plaything. To what extent can a man rule his own destiny? The sixteenth century was, after all, a period during which human beings were subject to incessant, often profound changes beyond their control: wars, revolutions, plagues, social unrest. Court life in particular was an uncertain means of existence, when a statesman might fall from power, or a queen be executed (Henry VIII's wives). But a belief that there was a benevolent Providence was a consolation. Many other writers of the age were preoccupied with speculations on this theme, including Shakespeare.

An important source for Kochanowski's philosophical and reflective epigrams was Seneca, whose plays contain many speculations on matters such as Fortuna, the brevity of life, death which spares no one, and the inevitability of growing old.[8]

VI *The Priapean God*

Like the epigrammatists of the *Greek Anthology*, not to mention certain Latin authors (Martial, Catullus, Propertius),

Kochanowski could turn his poetic art to producing verses bordering on the obscene. Of course, sixteenth-century obscenity was different from twentieth-century pornography. The Spanish doctor is again made a butt (II, 49):

> I don't have to find out,
> Whither you go, doctor, to make love;
> For any woman who indulges you of an evening,
> Reeks next morning of musk.

> Nie trzeba mi się wiele dowiadować,
> Kędy ty chodzisz, doktorze, milować,
> Bo która z tobą wieczór pobłaznuje,
> Każda nazajutrz piżmem zalatuje.

Commenting "On an old Man," Kochanowski writes that this individual suffered from priapismus, but was cured by "wise doctors." His wife then complained: "When you, my husband, suffered, I was healthy, / But now you are healthy, I shall fall sick" (II, 42). But the bawdry—as in the Latin and Greek poets —is rendered diverting by verbal skill; and for this, much can be forgiven.

CHAPTER 7

The Songs

KOCHANOWSKI'S lifelong devotion to the poets of classical antiquity has been mentioned and has indeed long been a subject of scholarly inquiry in Polish literary history.[1] Though most apparent, of course, in his Latin poetry, the indebtedness can also be seen in the Polish poetry, especially the *Songs* (published posthumously, 1586). But in addition to the presence of Horace, Catullus, and Propertius, among others, that of Petrarch is also strongly to be felt. Petrarch's lyrical poetry formed a vital link, after all, between the Latin poets and the Renaissance—not only in Italy, but all over Europe. The literary movement which took the name "Petrarchism," however, meant different things to poets who admired him in the fifteenth and sixteenth centuries. By the time Kochanowski was composing his *Songs,* the Petrarchan song-book (*canzoniere*) had become fossilized. Indeed, Petrarch's celebrated theory of love, in which his beloved Laura became a reflection of the Divine seen in its eternal aspect, had lost its validity; the usual reaction occurred, and the anti-Petrarchan school of poets appeared. An example of this school was John Donne, who satirized carnal love from the spiritual point of view, and spiritual love from the carnal. By the 1580's, certainly, Petrarch had largely been displaced in the imagination of poets by Ovid, the poet of frankly carnal love. However, Kochanowski wrote his songs at intervals throughout his creative life, and consistency of attitude is not to be looked for in them, any more than in the epigrams. The first song printed was that mentioned in chapter 3, of 1564. The collection was thus composed over two decades.

Unfortunately, Kochanowski left no statement defining what he meant by the term "song." The genre is, in any case, ill-defined, except that the word implies adaptation to music and

93

poetry "measured to the lyre," or sung. We have no record of Kochanowski's songs being sung; but then, we have no record of the *Carmina* of Horace being sung, though the title suggests that they were. Perhaps the word "lyre" and its derivative "lyrical" provide a clue.

About half the songs in Kochanowski's collection are translations, paraphrases, or imitations of Horace.[2] Oddly enough, Horace's poetry—though known—was not greatly admired during the Italian Cinquecento, thus Kochanowski's devotion did not derive from literary fashion. Clearly, this was the result of his own personal taste. The presence of Horace is to be felt more particularly in choice of themes, tone, and artistry. But the easy colloquialism of Horace can at times give way to a more elevated style. All the same, he succeeded in transplanting Horace to Polish soil.

I   *Chronology*

Just as the order in which Kochanowski composed his Polish epigrams is not known, and probably never will be, so the order in which he wrote the songs is equally obscure. But there are two main kinds—love songs and reflective songs, the latter including those with a religious, even hymnlike tone. Perhaps the love songs emanated from his period in Italy and at court, the others while he was living at Czarnolas. This, however, is speculation and, even if confirmed, adds nothing to our appreciation of them.

II   *Love Songs*

As with the Latin poetry, so with the Polish songs, scholars have long pondered whether they can be taken as evidence of personal experience. During the past fifty years or more, literary criticism and history have passed through different stages with regard to this pseudoproblem. At one time, the songs were regarded as Kochanowski's "lyrical memoirs." Portions of his biography were reconstructed on the basis of the poetry, most interest being devoted to his love affairs and married life. We have seen that the epigrams were also subjected to this kind of investigation. The next stage was investigation of Kochanowski's possible sources. Were his personal feelings and experience involved in their composition? At last, almost everything he wrote seemed to be little more than an artistic exercise or an imitation at best.[3] But, as we know, the reading of another man's poetry may in itself be a creative experience for a poet. Old-fashioned notions of "influence" are now seen as excessively simplifying the creative process.

Kochanowski's love songs present a special problem of language, as do those of Horace. His declarations of love for various ladies are usually worded so conventionally that they border on travesty. Horace often produces the same effect, as he well knew; he could simultaneously proclaim the intensity of his feelings, and urge us not to believe in them (the Phyrrha ode, I, v, "Quis multa gracilis," for example).[4] Likewise, Horace uses the conventional *exclusus amator* (a lover shut out), only to deride the situation when his mistress refuses to admit him—by threatening to walk away (III, 10). He is coolly aware of the absurdity of his own inflamed importunities. Kochanowski also uses the theme (I, 21) and combines it with another ancient theme, that of the *alba* (dawn):[5] a lover describes his night-long vigil at the door of his mistress' house, begging her to take pity on him and complaining "You sleep, while I outside / Since dusk / Suffer nocturnal inclement weather." He asks her to listen to the "violent rain, mixed with hail," assures her his intentions are not to rob her, and invokes Orpheus in a twelve-line digression. At last, the lover tells his unrelenting mistress that the bells of a nearby monastery are chiming, and as he leaves, he declares: "Good night, if anyone be listening, / Let my wreath in this ill-omened silence / Hang until dawn, / Witness of my lack of sleep."

A somewhat similar situation occurs in I, 25, except that here the door itself speaks, complaining of being badly treated by the importunate lovers of a harlot, as they seek entrance: "No night passes / Without my receiving cruel blows / From shameless drunkards; not to mention their language." The door "suffers through no fault of mine, / My depraved mistress is the cause of everything." Another *exclusus amator* appears, who "weeps night after night over me / Not letting me sleep with his mournful complaints" and reproaches the door that he is obliged to use the "cold threshold" as a bed, while the winds bear away his voice. Finally, the door comments that the *exclusus amator* will remain "all night long, until the cocks crow." The situation is based on an elegy of Propertius, but variations on this and the *alba* theme recur throughout Greek and Latin poetry, where excluded lovers spend nights of noisy desperation, beating on the doors of their mistresses, often receiving rough treatment by gatekeepers and rarely, if ever, being admitted. The weather is invariably harsh; cold winds and rainstorms occur every night.

A set of four "joyful" and three "unhappy" love songs within the collection may be associated with experiences Kochanowski had in Padua. All seven seem to be concerned with the same lady, though her identity is as irrelevant to the poetry as the identities of the various ladies addressed in the epigrams.

As in many of the epigrams on love, the language is often conventional to such a degree that it is at times difficult for a twentieth-century reader of poetry to admire the songs to the full. The poet speaks of his mistress in terms such as the "golden arrow" with which "unerring Love" has wounded him, but which causes his heart "inexpressible joy." More almost Baroque "conceits" follow: "It is no servitude to serve; but to serve him / Who is ungrateful of your services, that is equal / To the greatest unhappiness," and he thanks Love for preserving him from this fate (I, 4).

Almost in the same breath, the poet bids farewell to his mistress as she departs on a voyage: "Although your journey, dear one, pains me greatly, / I do not wish to restrain you against your will," and wishes her well; at the same time, however, he warns her "See what winds are rising, / How the clouds roll in the sky," and quotes the tale of "unfortunate Europa," captured by the infatuated god Zeus, who took the form of a bull and carried her off to Crete. Europa bitterly regretted leaving her native land, and the poet trusts that his mistress will not be a prey to similar regrets (I, 6).

The next song is a variation on the theme of departure: "It is time to part, / To abandon my joys and lute," because his mistress is leaving him. He envies the woods and cliffs which will see and hear her, while he himself will be mourning. Nothing is left to the poet but hope, for "Men reap in hope, and in hope they sow" (I, 7).

The poet reproaches "inviolate Neta," who shuns him, and compares her to a roe deer which, "when lost, / Seeks its mother amidst the steep mountains, / Not without fear and vain terrors." He expands the simile: "Were the leaves to move at all on a tree, / Or lizards stir in the undergrowth," then the timid creature would kneel in alarm. But the poet is no bear or "revengeful lioness," and tells Neta that it is time to cease following her mother, and take a husband (I, 11).

No collection of sixtenth-century love songs would be complete without at least one treating of the inconstancy of woman, and Kochanowski asks why women are so fickle that "they change like a summer breeze." Formerly, he was accounted "among the fortunate" and could obtain everything from his mistress; but "Today other winds blow against me, I have lost everything along with hope." He does not reproach her for preferring someone else, but warns her not to trust "he who admires beauty, / For he is building on feeble foundations." In her last hour, he would still be her friend, "though I prefer for you to weep over my grave" (I, 15).

Mythological allusions help make a point (II, 2) when the poet tells "Hanna," to whom the song is addressed: "I care not if the cold rocks / Dance at my singing"; if he gains her favors, he will have surpassed Amphion, a son of Zeus, whose playing caused the stones of Thebes to form fortifications for the city by their own volition.

Kochanowski celebrates married love (II, 10), pointing out that although a man may acquire fame in battle, or by his eloquence in peace time, if his wife is not adornment to him "the husband works in vain." The same principle applies in farming or trade: without his wife's help, all will be lost. Indeed, the wife is the "most reliable support of the home," and she is the "crown of her husband's head." She wards off troubles, and can ease his cares "with sweet words." She bears children who resemble their father (!) and he whom the Lord blesses with this union is "thrice joyful," though a "bad mate / Takes away everything."

When summoned by Bishop Myszkowski, a patron of the poet and one of the most wealthy magnates in Poland, to his residence near Krakow, Kochanowski politely complains of being obliged to leave his "little children and anxious wife" in order to make the journey. He reminds the bishop that Dorota must now take all the responsibility of his household, and he expresses the hope that neither will be separated again until death (II, 20).

This account of Kochanowski's love songs demonstrates that the varieties of love have not changed since the sixteenth century—nor, indeed, since man began recording experiences. Idealized, sexual, or married love are present everywhere in European poetry for two thousand years. To be sure, the establishment's view of what love ought to be changes from one generation to the next, and from one society to another. Today, perhaps, Freud is a greater authority on the subject than was Ovid to Kochanowski.

Love poetry of the Renaissance is essentially impersonal, whether it be in Polish, English, French, or Italian. There is no physical presence of the lady and, for all we know, the ladies themselves may well have been imaginary, the lover's situation imitated from earlier poets. Love is a central theme on which countless variations were played, with elegance, ingenuity, and often a subtly ironical tone.

III *The Philosopher*

Kochanowski's epigrams have already made clear his fondness for philosophizing in poetry. As in them, a well-worn Horatian or Senecan truth often sufficed for theme—the concept of originality is something comparatively new. But later in his life, Kochanowski was faced with more metaphysical questions: "What is the meaning of life?" "Who am I?" "What is Fortuna?" and the like.

Epicurean philosophizing finds a place during the Czarnolas period of retirement from the world. Epicurus (who died in 270 B.C.) held that the absence of pain is the greatest good; and since virtue produces this state of mind, man should pursue it. In his view moderation, friendship, and a simple life were the principles by which a rational man should live out his days.

Kochanowski evidently agreed, urging his readers to make the
best of fleeting moments and be satisfied with their lot, "for
who is so wise as to guess, / What will befall us tomorrow."
Only God knows "future things, and He laughs from Heaven /
When a man frets more than is necessary . . ." and "Everything is so strangely tangled / In this poor world of ours" (I, 9).

In the songs, as in the epigrams, Kochanowski also broods on
the mystery of Fortuna, by which everything is ruled. The
apparent indifference, even cruelty, of Fortuna toward man
never ceased to amaze Kochanowski, as they did Shakespeare,
who complained that "Each man is a fool to God" and "Some
unknown foe confuses human affairs." Neither poet solved the
mystery; perhaps the closest way to a solution was through Stoic
resignation, a kind of negative freedom.

Oddly enough, Fortuna was the only pagan deity who survived into the Renaissance without being in some way degraded,
as the other pagan gods and goddesses were. Indeed, a great
deal of respect continued to be paid to her throughout sixteenth-
century Europe by poets and philosophers. She represented
for them a universal, almost omnipotent power, and she "comes
into full vigor as an appropriate embodiment of underlying
paganism and superstition of the time."[6]

The alternative was perhaps to be found in the cultivation
and practice of virtue, that "eternal treasure" and "valuable
gem" (II, 3). Moderation, too—that Horatian virtue—is always
to be sought: "He who has daily bread / As much as man
needs, / Need not care for great sums / Or estates, towns and
lofty castles" (I, 5). After all, "Everything will remain / After
your death, my lord!" (I, 5).

Kochanowski even advises the reader "not to believe in Fortune, who sits on high" and to keep a watchful eye upon her,
"for she is a fickle woman by nature, and is often pleased to
alter matters." Gold is not to be trusted either: "Fortune, which
gives it, can take it away." But "virtue is an eternal treasure,"
a costly jewel "which enemies cannot seize, nor fire con-
sume" (II, 3).

Wine, too, is a consolation: "Do we wish to rejoice? / Command, my lord, your servants, / Let them bring good wine to
the table" (I, 9); or the poet addresses a wine-flask: "O my

painted wine-flask! / O my glazed wine-flask, / Whether there be weeping, or merriment, or fierce war, / Whether you bring love or tranquil slumber...," the poet will nevertheless pour wine for his guests. Even philosophers have been known to drink wine, despite their "heads full of wisdom" (I, 3). The theme reappears (I, 24) after a lengthy meditation on man as "God's plaything"—all man's cares disappear when wine is brought, from which "cheerful thoughts spring; / And care washed down with wine / Melts away like heated snow!" (I, 25).

IV *Mythology*

Like his contemporaries in Poland and elsewhere, Kochanowski found classical mythology an inexhaustible source of symbols. The gods and goddesses of antiquity are not mere ornament. Venus, Mars, Apollo, and the rest of the Olympians who crowd his poetry possessed, for the poet and his readers, innumerable associations with earlier poetry. Of course, neither Kochanowski nor his sixteenth-century readers believed in these figures; probably the Romans did not, either. Yet the ancient myths continue even today to exert their inexplicable fascination for poets and readers. In the sixteenth century, they occupied a place in a poet's technical equipment on a par with symbolism and other devices in the poetry of the twentieth century.

Orpheus and his lute, mourning Eurydice who has descended into the nether regions, is still a familiar figure, as Jean Cocteau knew when he produced a filmed version of the myth. Kochanowski and his audience were familiar with the myth. The Polish poet sums up Orpheus in a song lamenting the death of a palatine's wife, and the "loss of a kind friend and wife." Kochanowski attempts to console the palatine (who may have been a member of the illustrious Radziwiłł family) by reminding him that "Patience is best in this; / Unhappiness will find salvation with time." Even if the palatine were to take the lute of Orpheus and "visit the gloomy underworld / Where the sun's rays never appear; / You would not win back a soul which has once touched the water / Of that immemorial spring" (II, 6).

The incomparable musician Amphion, son of Zeus, has already been mentioned (I, 21), and the myth of Europa carried off by Zeus. But, in addition to the classical myths, Kochanowski also introduces Polish mythology, listing Lech the Slav, who "first settled in this land, / And ruled with his courage the powerful / Northern coasts," then Krak, the legendary founder of the city of Cracow (Krakow), with his daughter Wanda. Another mythical prince was Przemysl, who is said to have defeated his enemies by a "painted army" stratagem. Yet other legendary characters include Piast, a wheelwright who founded the Piast dynasty, and his son Zemowit. The song ends with a plea to the present ruler, King Zygmunt August, last of the Jagellonian dynasty, to hand over royal power to his son when he reaches old age (I, 10). That the king did not do so contributed to the disappearance of the Jagellons.

V *Pastoral Poetry*

In all periods of political or social unrest, poets have sought to construct the picture of an age not debased by corruption of royal courts and the vices of urban society. The closest they could come to this ideal state was, of course, the countryside: so we find Horace retiring from Rome to his Sabine farm, Kochanowski at Czarnolas, and in the eighteenth century His Grace Ignacy Krasicki, Bishop of Warmia, who lived thirty years in retirement, writing and cultivating his garden, while Alexander Pope withdrew from London to Twickenham for the same purposes.

In one of the best known of his songs, Kochanowski pictures the "dream of a simple life." It is summer; "The sun burns, the earth is almost turned to ashes, / The world is unrecognizable for dust" (a phrase applicable to Central Poland on occasion at the present day!). The rivers are running low, the vegetation calls upon Heaven for rain. But the poet has a remedy: the children are sent for cooled wine stored in a well, the table is placed under Kochanowski's celebrated leafy linden tree, and the poet's lute consoles him. Leafy shade, cool wine, poetry—all materials from which songs have been made since antiquity. The implication of this kind of poetry is, of course, that the poet is privileged to lead such a life undisturbed because of his vocation.

VI   *"Saint John's Eve"*

The "pastoral fallacy" inspired Theocritus, writing his idylls in the Greek island of Sicily in the second century B.C. Virgil had sung of it in Augustan Rome, with his *Eclogues*. The concept was not unknown in the Middle Ages. It is fundamentally pagan, and so is Kochanowski's cycle of twelve poems, known as "St. John's Eve," which bring the two books of songs to a conclusion. The poems celebrate Midsummer's night (June 24), with its attendant rites and ceremonies. These continue to be performed to the present day, in a modified form.

Pastoral poetry from Theocritus onward, depicting a remote country landscape populated by singing shepherds and their loves, is a poetic fantasy that has, on occasion, resulted in fine poetry. The pastoral tradition has always been creative, the voices of the shepherds being those of the poet himself. But, there is usually deliberate indifference to any of the more profound issues of human life. Each poet clearly believed that the chief value of his verses was to divert his readers by exquisite music and beauty of setting.[7]

Such poetry is always highly stylized, no matter how simple its surface may appear. For the pastoral convention implies a sophisticated poet and an audience sufficiently civilized to appreciate simplicity, which simple people rarely do. The audience is expected to recognize, too, that the gain of Art means the loss of Nature. Indeed, the "simple folk" of pastoral poetry are themselves idealized, and have few if any genuine roots in, or associations with, the crude, sometimes brutal reality of peasant life.[8]

Kochanowski's cycle of songs, each sung by a rustic maiden, has rightly been called his most Slavic work.[9] Unlike the epigrams and songs, the cycle was not intended for his learned patrons and friends, but for the delight of women. Perhaps he felt that women were more likely than men to feel the subtlety of these pastoral songs; or he may have been following Martial, who introduced his fifth book of epigrams by declaring: "Ladies, boys and little girls / This book is dedicated to you ... It is one that Domitian can pick up, / To read with the virgin Athena / looking on, and never blushing" (V, ii).

There is some doubt as to when the cycle was composed.
Most probably Kochanowski wrote the poems between 1567
and 1579. Internal evidence suggests their production soon after
the poet returned to his Czarnolas estate, after attending the
St. John's Eve rites which the cycle celebrates. Not that the
rites were unfamiliar to him; his childhood years spent in
Sycyna, where the rites were held annually as elsewhere, must
have left their mark in his imagination.

VII   *The Rites*

Professor Ulewicz has pointed out that the St. John's Eve rites
have their origin in pagan, prehistorical times, and they were
celebrated all over the lands of the Slavs. They were the sur-
vivals of a pagan cult of the sun. In debased form such rites
exist even in the present, although those who celebrate them in
Warsaw, Cracow, and elsewhere in Poland on Midsummer night
are probably not aware of their ancient origins.

The rites were widespread, and not restricted to Slavic countries. They have many names: in Germany, they are the *Johannis-
feuer*; in France, *le feu du St. Jean*; in Italy, the *Fuochi di San
Giovanni*. All may look back to the *ambarvalia* of Ancient Rome,
which included purification of fields, a solemn circumambula-
tion of fields in a procession, with bonfires and feasting outdoors, accompanied by prayers.

Fire continues to play the main part in the ceremonies and
rites. Young men light bonfires, and circle fields with burning
straw. Girls cast wreaths into the Vistula, or a nearby river. Then
the young men leap over the bonfires, or dance singing in a
ring. The essential element is lighting a bonfire at dusk, which
country folk say dispels sickness from cattle and purifies
the fields.

In Kochanowski's time, the rites were more elaborate. The
participants were not only the local folk, but also the inhabitants
of the manor house (gentry). The ceremonies lasted all night,
and included dancing (when various supposedly magical herbs
were worn), singing, music, revelry, and even fortune-telling.
Cattle were driven through the bonfires, to purify them.

Needless to say, the Catholic Church viewed these ceremonies with misgiving, partly because of their clearly pagan origins, partly because there is evidence that the participants took advantage of the occasion to misbehave. Sermons were preached against them, bishops issued prohibitions in the fourteenth and fifteenth centuries. Witchcraft was suspected. The Baroque poet Kasper Twardowski inveighed against them: "The folk, blinded with simplicity / Celebrate these disgusting superstitions. . . . These are not Christian rites at all, / The devil invented them, they are his errors." In the eighteenth century, Andrzej Kitowicz, recalling the pagan origins of the rites, records cases of young men colliding over bonfires, with accidents and conflagrations. Objections were still being raised by the Church as late as the middle of the nineteenth century. The Protestants were as eager as the Catholics to suppress the pagan revelries.

Kochanowski's cycle begins as the lights of the bonfires of St. John's Eve appear at dusk near Czarnolas, and local people and guests "hasten to the fire." The bonfire illuminates an area suitable for dancing and the seating of spectators. Three bagpipes (*baki*) start playing, and six pairs of maidens appear, dressed alike and adorned with herbs, mugwort (*belica*) especially being known for its magical properties. They join hands and the first maiden begins her song.

All the songs are serious in character and tone, for the rites the maidens are celebrating were known to have their origin in ancient tradition, handed down from one generation to the next. The first maiden reminds her hearers of this: "So our mothers handed down to us, / That which they themselves had from theirs." Nor should the ceremonies be hurried: "Today has come the time, when outdoors / We're to await the dawn." The dancing begins slowly, gradually gaining in tempo with the rhythm of the music, which includes a drum. Solemn though the rites are, laughter and joking accompany the dancing.

The second maiden admits she is fond of dancing (*tancuje barzo rada*), reminding her audience that everybody has some fault or other. She urges the other maidens to follow her in a circle, as she sings of her joy.

The third maiden takes up the refrain: "Follow me, follow me, delightful circle." "Man," she sings, is the "only being who can laugh," while all other creatures are dumb, so "let us laugh!"

The fourth maiden sings of love. This is a fine night, after all, and love is one of the oldest themes of poetry. She launched a wreath on the river, thinking of her lover Szymek; but she fears one of her companions may steal him from her. Indeed, the fifth maiden admits to an infatuation for the unfaithful swain Szymek, who has sought her hand in marriage. But now she regrets her "stupidity" in trusting him, and she knows that he is a "weed," not an herb. Szymek is known in the region for his inconstancy.

The sixth maiden is more practical, reminding the other maidens that "hot days are coming," and cattle seek the shade, followed by shepherds who "arouse tears by their playing." Harvesting is nigh. Not until the fields have been reaped will the folk rest and receive guests in a hospitable Polish way.

The dancing continues in a circle, but the seventh maiden complains that her lover prefers to hunt or drink, rather than dance with her. She mourns his absence from the rites, for her heart "always yearns for him"; she would prefer to enjoy his company in a "dense wood," and would assist him in the hunt. The eighth maiden also sings of love, complaining that her parents wish to marry her off though she is still young; the ninth weeps because her lover is unfaithful and she hides "inner wounds." Other singers are enumerated—the sailor "borne on sudden wind," "the poor ploughman / Though he almost swoons from laboring," "a nightingale on a poplar," mourning the fate of Ovid's Philomena transformed into a bird. Kochanowski digresses to narrate the myth (lines ten to twenty-four), and the maiden expresses satisfaction that such things do not happen in Poland. The tenth maiden also grieves: her lover has gone to the wars and she would fain accompany him, for she too would "grow accustomed to arms," while "let he who fears, perish!" In conclusion she urges him to "remember the oath you made to me."

The songs of the last two maidens differ in tone from those preceding them. The eleventh maiden celebrates the beauty of Dorota, later Kochanowski's wife, with her "face like mingled flowers / Lily and pink," and forehead "like polished marble," "coral lips," and "pearly teeth"—epithets now the height of convention, but symbolizing perfection for Renaissance and Baroque poets. Some of Kochanowski's "conceits" are almost Baroque:

"When I kiss you, / I taste sugar in my mouth for three days."

The song of the twelfth maiden is celebrated: "O tranquil countryside, and merry, / What voice can sing your praises?" The maiden enumerates the pleasures of a rural existence, with its ploughing, orchards, bee-keeping, harvesting, rustic songs, riddles, and dancing around the hearth in autumn, hunting and fishing, while the shepherd plays his flute and the "woodland fauns caper" (A faunowie skaczą leśni). Meanwhile the housewife prepares supper and helps her husband "as best she can." But now, as she sings, "day is here," and the ceremonies draw to an end.

VIII   *Folklore*

Despite his knowledge of the rites of St. John's Eve, Kochanowski does not mention the traditional casting of wreaths into a river (though he refers to it elsewhere). Moreover, his estate at Czarnolas was not situated on a river, and the third maiden sings "Here we are far from water." Furthermore, Kochanowski himself was evidently unaware of the pagan elements in the rite, since the first maiden urges those present to preserve it. Nor does the poet mention young men leaping through the bonfires, nor the driving of cattle through fires in a purification ceremony.

Historians of Polish literature have spent many years speculating whether Kochanowski's sources for the cycle were "national" (folklore) or "classical." There are plausible arguments for both views: the maidens quote Polish folk sayings, and Kochanowski provides the time and place:

> When the sun warms the Crab,
> And the nightingale sings no more,
> The fires of St. John's eve, as time befits
> Have been lit in Czarnolas.

> Gdy słońce Raka zagrzewa,
> A słowik więcej nie śpiewa,
> Sobotkę jako czas niesie,
> Zapalono w Czarnym Lesie.

On the other hand, the descriptive passages in the cycle are "general," as though Kochanowski did not regard the folk rites as worthy of more detailed description. Some scholars suggest an Italian origin in the "rusticale," or folk eclogues; but others disagree.

Be this as it may, Kochanowski's cycle is almost certainly Slavic in origin; even the eight-syllabic line which Kochanowski uses is a favorite meter for Slavic folk songs (not only Polish). Also, the simplicity, the deliberate archaisms, "unlearned" poetic diction, and relatively few run-on lines all point to folk poetry.

IX *The Idyll*

Kochanowski's cycle is an exploration at a consciously literary level of a theme which has humble origins—the pagan ceremonies of St. John's Eve. Despite its lowly origins, however, Kochanowski evidently felt—like Theocritus in his *Idylls* of the second century B.C.—that he could only give full expression to his creative impulse by a number of poems, not just one.[10] The same would apply in his *Laments* (next chapter). Yet the world of St. John's Eve and the twelve maidens is as narrow, even limited, as the world of the shepherds of Theocritus. Both cycles present a series of small scenes, not large panoramas, and this smallness of scale gives both their compact intensity. The range of characters in Kochanowski's cycle is even more circumscribed than that of Theocritus, for all the Polish maidens apparently belong to low social ranks. But the Greek and the Polish poet, seventeen centuries apart, both discerned a unique value in simplicity of feeling and directness of expression.

Kochanowski was one of the most sophisticated poets of his age in Poland, and founded with his St. John's Eve cycle what was to become a central poetic genre in Polish literature—the pastoral, with its variation, the idyll. The difference between the two kinds is mainly one of form; pastoral poetry rarely has formal structure, and indeed often becomes merely a vehicle for the poet's digressions. The idyll, however, properly speaking, takes the form of a contest of song (e.g., between shepherds, with a third character to act as judge).[11] So, in Polish poetry, we find pastorals or idylls in the seventeenth century (Baroque), in the Neo-classical, and Romantic periods, culminating in *Pan Tadeusz* of Adam Mickiewicz (1834), the epitome of Romantic poetry.

X *Descriptions*

In his many descriptive passages in the songs and "St. John's Eve" (and, indeed, elsewhere in his poetry), Kochanowski does not attempt the lengthy and detailed descriptive passages of observation of Rej. For the most part, they are brief passages introduced into the reflective lyrics for the purpose of stressing his own feelings or attitudes. There are no colorful descriptions of gardens or landscapes; rather, we find much the same kind of descriptive passages as in Latin poetry, in which landscapes are rarely considered at length.

A typical description of Nature occurs in the song already quoted briefly (I, 2), where the contrast of Winter and Spring serves as a starting point for the poet to reflect on philosophical and moral questions:

> The heart swells up, observing these times!
> Only lately, the forests were bare,
> Snow lay on the ground a yard deep,
> And the heaviest of carts ran across the rivers.
>
> Now the trees have taken leaves,
> The meadows have flowered beautifully,
> The ice has gone, and over the clear water
> Go the ships and carved boats.
>
> Now all the world smiles,
> The corn rises, a western wind blows.
> The birds ponder their nests
> And start to sing before daybreak.

> Serce rości patrząc na te czasy!
> Mało przed tym gołe były lasy,
> Śnieg na ziemi wyższej łokcia leżał,
> A po rzekach wóz nacięższy zbieżał.

Teraz drzewa liście na się wzięły,
Polne łąki, pięknie zakwitnęły;
Lody zeszły, a po czystej wodzie
Idą statki i ciosane łodzie.

Teraz prawie świat się wszystek śmieje,
Zboża wstały, wiatr zachodny wieje;
Ptacy sobie gniazda obmyślają,
A przede dniem śpiewać poczynają.

The first two stanzas describe the same phenomena in winter, then in spring. In effect, Kochanowski has selected three elements for comparison: the forests, meadows, and rivers, which he describes very economically. In winter, the trees are "bare," leafless, the meadows deep in snow, the rivers frozen over. But in spring, the same landscape changes: the forests become green, the meadows bloom, boats course the rivers. Although the poet does not express any feelings with regard to this change, the winter landscape is clearly less agreeable than that of spring. The predominance of nouns (thirteen in the nominative case, eight in oblique cases, i.e., twenty-one altogether), with only five adjectives and fourteen verbs lends solidity to the poem. It is almost prose, yet Kochanowski makes it memorable poetry. Similarly in the song:

Look now upon the forests,
How during the winter
The trees have lost all their beauty,
And snow covers high the fields.

Soon the spring will come,
This snow will suddenly vanish,
And the earth, when the sun warms it,
Will again be garbed in various colors.
                                              (II, 9)

Patrzaj teraz na lasy,
Jako prze zimne czasy
Wszystkę swą krasę drzewa utraciły,
A śniegi pola wysoko przykryły.

Po chwili wiosna przyjdzie,
Ten śnieg z nienagła zyjdzie,
A ziemia, skoro słońce jej zagrzeje,
W rozliczne barwy znowu się odzieje.

The same theme occurs as in the previous poem—contrast
between winter and spring. But this time the descriptions are not
so extended. On the other hand, the syntax is more complicated,
with subordinate clauses not found in the previous song. Nouns
occur six times in the nominative case, and six in oblique cases;
there are only two adjectives and seven verbs. But the elements
are the same (forests, meadows), with several new ones (the
sun, colors).

Forests, meadows, and fields appear in II, 2: "Now is the most
joyful time, / The forests are greening beautifully. / The meadows blossom variously." This landscape is extensive, ranging
over a panorama that includes the green forests, the flowering
meadows, and corn fields.

The Song of 1564, included in the collection of 1585, "Czego
chcesz od nas, Panie" (What would you of us, O Lord) (II, 25),
briefly describes the seasons as they follow each other, with the
flowers of spring, the harvesting of summer, the apples and
wine of autumn, and muddy winter—all in one four-line
stanza. Likewise in the first stanza of I, 14 (a paraphrase of
Horace's Ode I, 9):

> See, how the snow whitens on the mountains,
> > The winds rise from the north,
> > The lakes contract,
> The cranes, sensing winter, have flown away

> Patrzaj, jako śnieg po górach się bieli,
> > Wiatry z północy wstają,
> > Jeziora się ścinają,
> Żorawie, czując zimę, precz lecieli.

The elements here are: snow on the mountains, north winds,
frozen lakes, and the cranes flying away—of which neither the
north winds nor the cranes appear in Horace's ode. On several
occasions, Kochanowski starts a descriptive passage in the songs

by the imperative mood of "to look / behold" (patrzec), e.g., "Look now upon the forests" (II, 9); "Look how the snow shines white on the mountains" (I, 14); "The heart leaps up to behold these times" (I, 2).

One of Kochanowski's major contributions to the development of Polish poetry was his use of descriptions of nature, in language more artistic than that of Rej.

XI *"St. John's Eve"* in Manuscript

Professor Janusz Pelc (Warsaw) has published a description of the manuscript of "St. John's Eve" which is now in the Zamoyski library.[11] He suggests it may well be based on Kochanowski's own holograph, the more so as it contains textual variants differing from the posthumously printed version of 1586, which has been used for all later reprintings. As Professor Pelc reminds us, "devilishly few" of Kochanowski's manuscripts have survived. However, there exists an autograph letter in Polish, dating from 1571, in which Professor Pelc sees several similarities to the handwriting of the Zamoyski manuscript, and he bases his findings on them.

There appears to be a chronological relationship between "St. John's Eve" and a song (II, 2), which begins "I care not whether the cold rocks / Dance at my playing," and continues by inviting "Hanna" to Czarnolas. Is "Hanna" another name for his wife-to-be Dorota? We do not know, and the question is irrelevant to the poetry. But which poem came first? Kochanowski may have quoted himself in "St. John's Eve" from the song, or vice versa. The question remains one of the many questions, either of a biographical or bibliographical nature, still to be solved.

CHAPTER 8

The Laments

AROUND the year 1580, a great revival of the Catholic faith spread across Poland, as elsewhere in Europe, accompanied by a large-scale return to the more mystical aspects of religion. To be sure, Luther's doctrines of the Reformation had flowed across Poland, but it was a shallow stream; the peasantry and lesser gentry remained largely Catholic throughout the period, with a few exceptions such as Mikołaj Rej, the popular Calvinist of his time.

The return to mysticism in religion, encouraged by the missionary Jesuit order (Societas Jesu) and the Counter-Reformation movement of religious reform, was to prove a prologue to the appearance in European literature of the Baroque spirit, or style. In Poland, the Baroque spirit predominates until well into the eighteenth century (1601 to 1764 are useful, if approximate, dates for Polish Baroque in literature and all the arts—music, architecture, painting, and even landscape gardening).

Essentially, mysticism means that men turned to the spiritual aspects of their religion: they became less concerned with matters such as politics, power, or heroic deeds on the battlefield. Wars were no longer occasions when a king or prince led his men out to do battle; they became squalid wars, in which mercenaries hacked one another to pieces in the name of religion. There was a growing preoccupation with salvation, man's unworthiness, the practice of meditation as a means of communicating with God or the saints. The medieval cult of the Virgin Mary was revived (Kochanowski never refers to the Virgin Mary or any of the Christian saints).

Kochanowski's last major work, *Treny* (Laments, 1580), explores in poetical language man's relation with God. He composed the cycle of nineteen poems to lament the death in early childhood of a daughter, Ursula, who had died the previous year. The *Laments* are the most remarkable cycle of poems in Old Polish literature (to the 1820's) and were imitated many times by later writers. They have been admired and studied throughout the centuries, to the present day.[1]

The cycle is exceptional in Kochanowski's work. These poems are his most personal, even intimate poems—though they do not tell us as much as the epigrams. He composed them and had them printed within a year of the child's death. The rapidity of composition and printing differs greatly from his usual method of proceeding with other kinds of poetry. Both the collections of songs and epigrams were written over some thirty years, and not printed in his lifetime. The *Psalms* occupied him for nearly a decade. A possible exception is the play *The Dismissal of the Grecian Envoys*, though much of that work may have been composed considerably before its production.

The death of his child was clearly an event of such tragic dimensions to the poet that he was compelled to unburden his feelings and thoughts. Not, however, that he did so in the unrestrained outbursts of grief familiar in later poetry. His tone (as will be seen) remains that of the great classical utterances of the Roman poets. Yet the undercurrent of desolation and grief is always present.

His contemporaries admired the *Laments*, which were reprinted four times within the next five years—an extraordinary figure for the period. But the *Laments* did not receive the same kind of general approval as his other works, such as the *Psalms,* for they did not "echo great events" or "teach and console" the ordinary reader. Generally speaking, this view was current in Polish literary history until the end of the nineteenth century.

Two classes of readers existed in Poland in Kochanowski's time, as elsewhere in Europe: the intellectual elite, versed in Greek and Latin literatures, with a humanistic turn of mind and often cosmopolitan in outlook; and the great mass of the rural gentry, whose preferred and often only reading matter consisted of the Psalms, sermons, hymnals, and works of instruction such as *The Art of Choosing a Wife* and *How to Behave at Table.*

The intellectual elite was a numerically small class; but they were more influential in shaping literary taste. They criticized

the *Laments* because the cycle was a form unknown to the
Classical authors, and a mixed genre, varying from song to
epitaph. Elements from Christianity and the pagan authors,
especially Cicero, were mingled. Some of the poems can stand
alone, while others complement those preceding or following.
Even the epitaphs did not accord with Scaliger's rules for that
genre, which should consist of an orderly arrangement of panegyric of the dead person, a consolation, and finally an exhortation to the mourners. But Kochanowski was deliberately breaking away from such schematic arrangements, as a result of the
new trends of that time, and of his own poetic originality—even
though he could not break away from them entirely.[2]

I *The Poetry of Grief*

Death, or "the sleep that is due to all," has been the occasion
for more poetry than any other of the woes that afflict mankind. Arguments of all kinds have been used in attempts (always
vain) to console the bereaved: reason accepts that "death is
inevitable," that "all men have to die," that "death is payment
of a debt due to Nature," a release, the end of a journey. Death,
we are told, can be assuaged by recollecting past joys and even
by expressing grief.[3]

Kochanowski knew the "consolations" of antiquity. But all
proved inadequate when he himself was confronted with the
premature death of his own child. Conventional expressions of
grief were useless. His own grief was his theme, not a conven-
tionalized theme borrowed from antiquity. This in itself is one
measure of Kochanowski's originality in the cycle, especially
when we take the work within its period.

In effect, Kochanowski was seeking to communicate his
feelings; and as T. S. Eliot said, the expression of "precise emotion" requires as much intellectual power as the expression of
"precise thought," adding that "every precise emotion tends
towards intellectual formulation."[4] Thus, to write about or to
communicate an emotional state, whether it be that of love
or grief, is as difficult and concentrated a task as to describe
a mental process.

As mentioned above, the *Laments* are a cycle of nineteen

poems, ranging in length from fourteen to over one hundred and
fifty lines, in varying meters, and we may enquire in passing
why Kochanowski found himself obliged to compose nineteen
separate (although, of course, thematically unified) poems to
mourn the death of his child. He had mourned the death of
princes in a single threnody. The answer to this question will
become apparent as we examine the cycle in detail.

In terms of literary genres, the threnody or lament had considerable prestige, and had never been used in Polish poetry to
mourn the death of an unknown child; had Ursula been a princess, a threnody might have been appropriate. But the death of
a child is especially poignant, and there had been other forms
of artistic expression on such an occasion in the form of funeral
monuments, such as that erected by the Chancellor Szydlowiecki
for a young son, bearing the Latin inscription: "His most attached
father placed this monument to his son, as to a little flower that
had consoled his noble house." The Szydlowiecki monument
provided a model for other similar monuments on the tombs of
children in sixteenth-century Poland.[5]

II *Chronology*

As with all Kochanowski's collections of songs and epigrams,
we do not know in what order he composed the *Laments*. He
had, of course, written numerous epitaphs, e.g., the Epitaph to
a Child, in which the child seeks to console his mourning father,
and Latin epitaphs also, in which the poet declared he had
raised a monument to his children (Foricoenia 119, 120), in
which the monument speaks: "Here I stand, not like Niobe
who turned to stone on losing her children, / Though I too am
witness of children lost."

Although scholars have not been able to determine the order
in which Kochanowski wrote his *Laments*, their arrangement
and order in print are those of the poet himself, and form a
coherent entity. The first thirteen laments are expressions of
grief, even despair; the last six gradually reaffirm the Christian
precept which is synthesized in the final, and longest, of the
laments (XIX, The Dream), namely, "Thy will be done." The
cycle leads through all stages of grief, from initial despair to a

116 JAN KOCHANOWSKI

final acceptance of the inevitability of loss. Grief here is not a static condition, but an emotion in continual flux and change. Kochanowski describes how his emotions change with the passage of time as the cycle proceeds. He starts with a prose dedication:

To Ursula Kochanowska, a charming, delightful, gifted child who, having shown great promise of all the maidenly virtues and attributes, suddenly and unaccountably passed away in her infancy, to the great and unbearable grief of her parents. Written with tears by Jan Kochanowski, her unhappy father, to his dearest child. Ursula, thou art no more!

Orszuli Kochanowskiej, wdzięcznej, ucieszonej, niepospolitej dziecinie, która, cnót wszytkich i dzielności panieńskich początki wielkie pokazawszy, nagle, nieodpowiednie, w niedoszłym wieku swoim, z wielkim a nieznośnym rodziców swych żalem zgasła—Jan Kochanowski, niefortunny ociec, swojej namilszej dziewce z łzami napisał. Nie masz Cię, Orzulo moja!

The dedication is preceded by an epigraph from Cicero's Latin version of Homer's *Odyssey*: "For the mind in men upon earth goes according to the fortunes which the father of gods and men, day by day, bestows upon them." The significance of this reference to Jupiter (Zeus) is noted below.

III *Themes*

Four central themes are stated in the dedication: the "charming, delightful, gifted child," her "great promise," the bereaved parents, with their "great and unbearable grief," and absence of the child in death.

The first two laments are poetic meditations on these themes. Kochanowski appeals to Heraclitus of Ephesus (end of the sixth century B.C.), who mourned over the transitory nature of man's life, and Simonides (died 469 B.C.), an elegiac poet known in antiquity for his threnodies. "Cruel Death" has suddenly deprived the poet of "all my joys," like a serpent which,

> having seen a hidden nest,
> Takes the pitiful little nightingales, and feeds

His greedy throat; meanwhile, the unhappy mother
twitters, and hurls herself time and again
   on the murderer.
In vain!

Tak więc smok, upatrzywszy gniazdo kryjome,
Słowiczki liche zbiera, a swe łakome
Gardło pasie; tymczasem matka szczebiece
Uboga, a na zbójcę coraz się miece,
Próżno!

Others, says the poet, will tell him "Weeping is vain"—but
what, after all, is not vain in this world? "The life of man is
naught but vanity," and the lament ends with the question: "Ah,
which are better, then—to seek relief / In tears, or strive to
conquer grief?"

He has no subject for poetry now except the child's death,
for "Now disaster drives me on by force, / To songs unheeded
by the great concourse / Of mortals." Death, the "grimmest of
all maids, / Inexorable princess of the shades" has claimed the
child, and "Verses that I would not sing / The living, to the
dead I needs must bring." Her parents' grief recurs with the
thought that "all the joy a loving child should bring / Her
parents, is become their bitterest sting."

The bereaved father realizes, in the third lament, that nothing
is left for him but "only follow on / Along the path where earlier
thou had gone." The child was to have been his heiress, her
"future virtues" already being apparent. But now "you will
never return to me," though if God wills the poet will behold
her again "and you will clasp / Your father's neck with your
tiny hands!"

The theme that Ursula would have been his heiress, had she
lived, reappears in the next lament:

Had God granted to her ample days
I might have walked with her down flowering ways
And left this life at last, content, descending
To the realms of dark Persephone.

A ona, by był Bóg chciał, dłuższym wiekiem swoim
Siła pociech przymnożyć mogła oczom moim.

A przynajmniej tymczasem mogłem był odprawić
Wiek swój i Persefonie ostatniej się stawić.

Kochanowski continues to rail against "unholy Death," which
breathes pestilence or comes like a "busy gardener, weeding
out / Sharp thorns and nettles, cuts the little sprout. . . ." Thus
Ursula too perished: "In a little space she grew beside us here, /
Then Death came . . . and she / Fell stricken lifeless." Yet again,
the poet demands of Persephone: "This flow / Of barren tears,
how couldst thou will it so?"

The child appears as the "dear little Slavic Sappho" in Lament
VI. Again the poet sees her as she might have been, and promises
"thou shouldst have had a heritage one day / Beyond thy
father's lands." But "death came stalking by thee, timid thing, /
And thou in sudden terror tookest wing," and Ursula bade farewell to her mother (the parental grief theme), saying:

> My mother, I shall serve thee now no more
> Nor sit about thy table's charming store;
> I must lay down my keys to go from here,
> To leave the mansion of my parents dear.

> Już ja tobie, moja matko, służyć nie będę
> Ani za twym wdzięcznym stołem miejsca zasiędę;
> Przyjdzie mi klucze położyć, samej precz jechać,
> Domu rodziców swych miłych wiecznie zaniechać.

IV   The Death Wedding

A subtle change in the metrical pattern occurs in the next
lament (VII) from the already traditional thirteen-syllabic line
with the caesura after the seventh syllable or eighth (as in numbers V and VI: e.g., "Jako oliwka mała / pod wysokim sadem,"
and "Ucieszna moja spiewaczko! Safo słowieńska!) with regular couplets, to a pattern of thirteen-syllabic lines alternating
with seven-syllabic lines. Now he dwells on the child Ursula as
she had been when alive: "Sad trinkets of my little daughter,
dresses / That touched her like caresses, / Why do you draw
my mournful eyes?" Kochanowski introduces into this lament
the "death wedding" theme of Slavic folklore, in which a .girl

who died unmarried would traditionally be arrayed in bridal
garments before burial:

> My little girl, 'twas to a bed far other
>   That one day thy poor mother
> Had thought to lead thee, and this simple dower
>   Suits not the bridal hour;
> A tiny shroud and gown of her own sewing
>   She gives thee at thy going.
> Thy father brings a clod of earth, a somber
>   Pillow for thy last slumber.

> Nie do takiej łoźnice, moja dziewko droga,
>   Miała cię mać uboga
> Doprowadzić! Nie takąć dać obiecowała
>   Wyprawę, jakąć dała!
> Giezłeczkoć tylko dała a lichą tkaneczkę;
>   Ociec ziemie bryleczką
> W główki włożył—niestetyż, i posag, i ona
>   W jednej skrzynce zamkniona!

The "death wedding" theme occurs elsewhere in Polish poetry,
notably in one of the idylls of Bartlomiej Zimorowic (died *ca.*
1680), entitled "The Mourners" (*Narzekalnice*):

> My wedding dress—a winding-sheet;
> A handful of earth—my dowry,
> My bridegroom, the worm; the grave my marriage bed;
> My offspring—the tears of my parents.

> Garść ziemie—to mój posag; weselne odzienie
> Prześcieradło; wyprawa—trunna i kamienie;
> Robak—mój oblubieniec; grób—moja łoźnica;
> Potomstwo me—płacz krewnych i gorzka tesknica.

Even a cursory examination of this epitaph reveals an example of the total change that Polish poetry underwent in the
hundred years dividing the two poets. The absence of verbs
and connectives gives the lines a remarkable tension, intensified
by the powerful contrasts.

The "poetic diction" (words that draw attention to themselves) which Kochanowski employs in this lament is marked by frequent diminutives (czloneczki, letniczek, uploteczki, giezłeczko, bryleczka—words for which English has no equivalent). Such words have a particularly tender and affectionate tone in Polish, and were much used by admirers of Kochanowski in the Age of Enlightenment. Adam Naruszewicz employs them frequently in his idylls, where they were considered highly suited to that relatively "low" genre. But later writers derided this aspect of Naruszewicz's poetry, and his contemporary, Ignacy Krasicki, parodied them in his mock-heroic *Myszeidos* (Battle of the Mice, 1775).[6]

V *Search for Consolation*

Kochanowski reverts to the present in Lament VIII. Now, his house is but "an empty thing," rendered so by Ursula's death. The house is full, "yet as though there were no one." One tiny soul has deprived them of so much. When she was alive, Ursula "sang joyousness to all, / Running through every nook of house and hall." But now "all is silent, the house utterly deserted," and "all in vain the heart would seek relief."

Now Kochanowski turns to the philosophers of antiquity for consolation. He addresses Wisdom, which—if other people are to be believed—can uproot all passions and all human woes, and even change a man into an angel "which knows no pain, feels no woe, / Yields to no misfortune, pays no homage to fears." Wisdom does not fear Death, which she contemplates "unafraid, still calm, inviolate." But now Kochanowski calls himself "a hapless man ... who sought / If I might gain thy threshold by much thought," now cast down, "but one amid the countless throng."

The dream which is to conclude the cycle (Lament XIX) is foreshadowed in Lament X, as the poet asks the child:

> My dearest Ursula, say where
> Art thou departed, to what land, what sphere?
> High o'er the heavens wert thou brought, to stand
> A little cherub 'midst the cherub band?

Orzulo moja wdzięczna, gdzieś mi się podziała?
W którą stronę, w którąś się krainę udała?
Czyś ty nad wszytki nieba wysoko wniesiona
I tam w liczbę aniołków małych policzona?

No matter where Ursula may be—in Paradise, or the "Islands of the Blest," or crossing Lethe, the river of forgetfulness—the poet asks her "Art thou unwitting of my sore distress?" Has she, perhaps, been transformed into a nightingale? Or condemned to Purgatory? Wherever she may be, the poet pleads with her to take pity on his sorrow: "Console me as best you can, and appear to me / In a dream, or as a shade, or in nightmare!" This plea will be answered at the end of the cycle.

A question that recurs throughout Kochanowski's poetry is whether "Virtue is its own reward." For the most part, the poet assumes that it is; but in Lament XI he questions even this assumption, quoting Brutus in defeat, who said: "Virtue is but a name." The reference is to Cicero's *Tusculan Disputations*, addressed to Brutus, one of the assassins of Julius Caesar who killed himself after his defeat at Philippi in 42 B.C. Cicero quotes Greek philosophers "whose opinion it is that virtue has no power in itself," and who justified suicide as an escape from human ills.

In Brutus's phrase, Kochanowski uses the Polish word *fraszka*, one of the key words in his vocabulary, as Professor Weintraub demonstrated.[7] Sometimes the word denotes "epigram" (see chapter 5), sometimes a joke. In sixteenth-century English, the word "frask" meant a trick. In Lament XI, Kochanowski gives the word a note of powerful irony by coupling it with "virtue," and placing it in the mouth of Brutus, who was in many ways the embodiment of virtue for the Renaissance. He, after all, was the symbol of the Republican tradition in Rome, "the noblest Roman of them all," as Shakespeare's Julius Caesar called him. The Polish gentry of Kochanowski's time liked regarding themselves as incarnations or at least heirs of the Roman patricians under the Emperor Augustus (around the birth of Christ). To them, sixteenth-century Poland was a modern version of the Roman republic, and the association was maintained until late in the eighteenth century, as witness Ignacy Krasicki's treatise *The Squire* (1778–1802).[8]

Dismissing Virtue in a contemptuous (albeit quoted) phrase, the poet now muses that "Some unknown foe confuses men's affairs; / For good and bad alike it nothing cares." He derides man's attempts to penetrate the mystery of Heaven by means of his reason: "Light dreams, shallow dreams amuse us, / Though they will probably never come to pass" (another significant reference foreshadowing Lament XIX), and the grieving father challenges Grief: "Wilt thou blight / My powers of reason and my dear delight?"

The child Ursula reappears in Lament XII as she had been when alive: "unspoiled and neat, obedient at all times, / She seemed already versed in songs and rhymes." A range of epithets describes her as "Discreet and modest, sociable and free / From jealous habits, docile, mannerly." She said her prayers at morning and at night, even though she was but "thirty months" of age. But her youth could not endure so many virtues, and, like a "little ear of wheat," she fell to the reaper. Developing the metaphor, the poet buries both the child and his hopes in the "sorrowful ground," though she will never again "blossom before his mournful eyes."

In his continued grief, the poet next wishes (XIII) that his "charming Ursula" had either not died or not been born at all, for he is paying with his great grief and her departure for small consolations. Indeed, she deceived him like a "fleeting nocturnal dream" which cheats the dreamer's greed with "the magnitude of gold" but then disappears, leaving only "desire and longing." He continues to reproach the child for "arousing great hopes," then suddenly fleeing away, taking with her all his pleasure and "half my soul." He remains with nothing but "eternal longing," and an epitaph:

> Ursula Kochanowska lieth here,
> Her father's sorrow and her father's dear;
> For heedless Death hath acted here criss-cross;
> She should have mourned my death, not I her loss.

> Orszula Kochanowska tu leży, kochanie
> Ojcowe albo raczej płacz i narzekanie.
> Opakeś to, niebaczna śmierci, udziałała;
> Nie jać onej, ale mnie ona płakać miała.

Classical mythology as a poetic device, not mere ornamentation, reappears in Lament XIV.[9] Kochanowski's contemporaries would immediately have responded to the question with which this lament opens: "Where are those mournful gates, through which years ago / Orpheus went into the earth seeking his lost one?" The poet would follow the same pathway in search of his beloved daughter and cross "that ferry, across which / A stern guide conducts pale shadows." He would take his lute into the chambers of stern Pluto, so that it might persuade him "with mournful songs" and tears to let Ursula return to her father.

The poet again addresses his lute and Eratus, the god of lyrical poetry, from which "sorrowful men find consolation in their griefs" (XV). He implores them to "calm for a while my desperate mind / Before I turn into stone." He summons Niobe, asking, "Unhappy mother ... / Where are thy sons and daughters, seven of each, / The joyful cause of thy too boastful speech?" The myth was that Niobe boasted to Lantona, mother of Apollo and Diana, that she had had seven sons and daughters. Apollo and Diana, affronted, slew all Niobe's children, and she turned to stone from grief (Ovid, *Metamorphoses* vi, 301–312). Even so, "hidden wounds" lay beneath the stone, for her tears emerge from the rock and fall in "a transparent stream" of which animals and birds drink. But Niobe in "eternal bondage / Is rooted in the rock."

VI *Cicero and Job*

A change in the traditional metrical pattern of thirteen syllables, used by the poet in Laments VIII through XV, occurs in Lament XVI: now, the eleven stanzas in alcaics express his hesitant appeal to Classical philosophy, contrasting with the Christian philosophy to which he had turned in the earlier laments—but in vain.

He rejects his lute, and ponders whether he "sees true, or hath a dream / Flown forth from ivory gates to gleam / In phantom gold?" The "ivory gates" are those described by Penelope in the *Odyssey* (xix, 560–67): "for two are the gates of shadowy dreams, and one is fashioned of horn and one of ivory." Dreams from the ivory gates deceive men, but those from the gates of horn come true. He reproaches "mad, mistaken mankind," heedless, extolling the virtues of poverty when himself wealthy, and "Midst pleasures holding grief to be . . . a trifle." But when misfortune or sorrow occurs, man repines. Kochanowski provides an example of the futility of Stoic philosophy as expounded by Cicero in the *Tusculan Disputations,* where he urged the necessity for maintaining an even temper in times of joy and of sorrow. But even "eloquent Cicero" was made wretched by the death of his daughter and expressed his grief in letters to friends. Cicero's tragic situation foreshadowed that of Kochanowski, who asks him:

> Why dost mourn thy daughter so
> When thou hast said the only woe
> That man need dread is base dishonor?
> Why sorrow on her?

> Death, thou hast said, can terrify
> The godless man alone. Then why
> So loth, the pay for boldness giving,
> To leave off living?

> Czemu tak barzo córki swej żałujesz?
> Wszak się ty tylko sromoty wiarujesz;
> Insze wszelakie u ciebie przygody
> Ledwie nie gody!

> Śmierć—mówisz—straszna tylko niebożnemu.
> Przeczże się tobie umrzeć, cnotliwemu,
> Nie chciało, kiedyś prze dotkliwą mowę
> Miał podać głowę?

Finally, the poet appeals to Time, the "longed-for father of forgetfulness," to heal his "sorrowful heart, and this harsh grief / Remove from my mind!"

Having rejected the Classical philosophers, Kochanowski exclaims like Job in the Old Testament: "The hand of God has touched me" (xix, 21). His tone is that of the psalmist who lamented:

O Lord God of my salvation, I have cried day and night before thee.
Let my prayer come before Thee; incline Thine ear unto my cry; for
my soul is full of troubles, and my life draweth nigh unto the grave.

(Psalms, lxxxviii, 1–3)

There is another echo of the Psalms in lines 5–8 of this lament
(XVII): "For day and night Thy hand was heavy upon me;
my moisture is turned into the drought of summer" (xxxii, 4),
where the poet declares:

> If the sun doth wake and rise,
> If it sink in gilded skies,
> All alike my heart doth ache,
> Comfort it can never take.

> Lubo wstając gore jaśnie,
> Lubo padnąc słońce gaśnie,
> Mnie jednako serce boli,
> A nigdy się nie utoli.

Then comes an echo of Horace:

> Though we shun the stormy sea,
> Though from war's affray we flee,
> Yet misfortune shows her face
> Howsoe'er concealed our place.

> Próżno morzem nie pływamy,
> Próżno w bitwach nie bywamy:
> Ugodzi nieszczęście wszędzie,
> Choć podobieństwa nie będzie.

The reference is to *Odes* II, xiii: "Ille et nefasto," especially
lines 13–20:

What each man should shun is never duly guarded against; the
Carthaginian sailor trembles at the Bosphorus but dreads hidden fate
from another cause; a soldier dreads the arrows and swift flight of
the Parthian, who fears the fetters and dungeons of Italy; but the
unforeseen power of death has swept nations away, and will still
sweep them away.

The poet's life was so modest that "few there were could know my name," while "evil hap and jealousy / Had no way of harming me." Yet even this retired and modest life was of no avail when the Lord struck, "the more swiftly and surely / In that I was more secure."

He speaks ironically of "reason" (rozum) or philosophy, and there is a gradual change in tone as the poet admits "Wisdom, I most truly know, / Hath no power to console; / Only God can make me whole." Indeed, in the penultimate lament (XVIII) Kochanowski turns to God and declares in all humility that "We are Thy disobedient children, Lord." Eechoing Job again ("Though He slay me, yet will I trust in Him," xiii, 15), the poet admits that "in times of joy / We but rarely call on You." All comes from God's grace and mercy:

> I know Thy mercy doth abound
> And the world will perish,
> Before Thou condemn the humble . . .
> Great are my transgressions,
> But Thy mercy
> Surpasses all iniquities.
> Lord, manifest Thy mercy unto me this day!

> Ale od wieku Twoja lutość słynie,
>   A pierwej świat zaginie,
>   Niż Ty wzgardzisz pokornym . . .

> Wielkie przed Tobą są występy moje,
>   Lecz miłosierdzie Twoje
>   Przewyższa wszytki złości
> Użyj dziś, Panie, nade mną litości!

VII   *"To Justify the Ways of God to Man"*

The question "Why has God done this to me?" is a sadly familiar one. Poets have attempted to answer the question since Job was afflicted in the Old Testament. But their utterances are rarely logical or even philosophical by nature. If anything, the answer is to be found in a change of attitude. Job could find no logical answer as to why the Almighty caused his sons to be killed; instead, he distills a mood in poetry, by which a man finds he is able, despite all, to continue living.[10]

VIII   *Lament XIX* "The Dream"

Symbols of Death and Grief reappear throughout the cycle, along with references to sleep and dreams. The final, and longest, lament bears the title "The Dream" (no other lament has a title). As Dr. Peterkiewicz has shown, Kochanowski is here utilizing the "dream vision" formula well known to poets in the Middle Ages and Renaissance.[11] The formula was based on a celebrated classification of dreams made in the fourth century A.D. by Macrobius, a learned commentator on Classical texts, which he preserved during the Dark Ages. Indeed, he was one of that small but important number of European scholars directly responsible for preserving the traditions of antiquity in the liberal arts, philosophy ,and science, which they handed down in laboriously copied manuscripts to later generations.

The classification of dreams by Macrobius was in his commentary on Cicero's *Dream of Scipio,* which became one of the most influential books of the Middle Ages. Indeed, few other books of comparatively small size contained so much material which writers used. First printed in 1472, the commentary had some thirty editions within the next century, being printed in Paris, Venice, Lyons, and Cologne.

Macrobius differentiated among five classes of dreams, of which three classes were significant: prophetic dreams, enigmatic dreams requiring interpretation, and oracular dreams. In the last-named class, the dreamer is visited by a sacred person (such as a god or, in later periods, a priest) or a relative. The figure offers advice to the dreamer, and the advice is to be considered reliable. In Scipio's dream, as retold by Cicero, his late father appeared to him, indicating that this was a "true dream." In Kochanowski's lament, the figure of his late mother appears to him with the child. The implication is the same.

Of course, dreams have always interested man. The Old and New Testaments bear witness to this; the ancient Israelites recorded various dreams, believing them to be manifestations of Jehovah, or instruments of prophecy. Not only does Jehovah speak to Old Testament men in their dreams, but men can answer and hold long dialogues with Him. But the dreams are ephemeral, and the content is more important than the medium.

The dream vision as a literary device appears in the early English alliterative poem *The Pearl* (mid-fourteenth century). Its anonymous author's two-year-old daughter had died, but he was granted a dream vision of the child in Paradise and awoke, consoled. Chaucer's dreamer in the *Parlement of Foules* (1386?) saw the court of Nature in his sleep; while Boccaccio adopted the formula in his *Olimpia*, mourning the death of his daughter who appears to him in a dream.

IX *"The Dream"* (2)

In the first eighteen laments, only Ursula herself and her mother appeared. Now, the poet's own mother—who passed away twenty years earlier, and of whom we know nothing—appears in a dream and speaks to him. The poet passed the night mourning, only to fall asleep at dawn:

> And then it was my mother did appear
> Before mine eyes in vision doubly dear;
> For in her arms she held my dearest one,
> My Ursula, just as she used to run
> To me at dawn to say her morning prayer.

> Natenczas mi się matka właśnie ukazała,
> A na ręku Orszulę moję wdzięczną miała,
> Jaka więc po paciorek do mnie przychodziła,
> Skoro z swego posłania rano się ruszyła.

She speaks to him: "It is thy weeping brings me to this shore," for his lamentations have penetrated into the "hidden chambers of the dead." She questions him: "Dost thou believe the dead have perished quite, Their sun gone down in an eternal night?" This is the first argument the poet's mother uses in endeavoring to console him. She reminds him that Ursula is now living a happier life than on earth, and her soul is immortal, for she died in a state of grace: "the spirit, given / A life eternal, must go back to Heaven." The child, after all, "did not leave a land

of much delight, / But one of toil, and grief, and evil blight."
By her early death, Ursula "knew not the pangs that usher in /
The newborn child." She remained blissfully ignorant of misfortune, disaster, sickness, and death. In Heaven, "We live a
life of endless joy that brings / Good thoughts ... / The sun
shines on forever here, its light / Unconquered by impenetrable
night." Then, too, Ursula's premature death spared her from
the "ills of man's estate," such as the "pagan, shameful thrall"
of Tatar captivity in the Crimea—a theme that resounds through
Polish literature ever since the times of the first Tatar invasions
of the country up to Mickiewicz's *Crimean Sonnets* (1826) and
Sienkiewicz's *Trilogy.*
The third argument for consolation now appears:

> Be in this matter thine own lord, although
> Thy longed-for happiness thou must forego.
> For man is born exposed to circumstance,
> To be the target of all evil chance,
> And if we like it or we like it not
> We still cannot escape our destined lot.

> W tę bądź przedsię panem,
> Jako się kolwiek czujesz w pociechy obranem.
> Człowiek urodziwszy się zasiadł w prawie takim,
> Że ma być jako celem przygodom wszelakim;
> Z tego trudno się zdzierać!

> (109–113)

Yet again, Kochanowski is reverting here to the theme of
Fortuna, always a preoccupation of Renaissance man. His mother
reminds him as the dream proceeds that "the ways of God are
past our finding out, / Yet what He holds as good shall we mis-
doubt?" There is also an echo of the New Testament here, when
St. Paul cries: "O the depth of the riches both of the wisdom
and knowledge of God! How unsearchable are his judgments!"
(Romans xi, 33).
The poet's mother suggests a fourth consolation, reminding
him that misfortune has not singled him out with unusual malig-
nity, but "it lays its burdens upon everyone." Again,

Fortuna's power is such, my dearest son,
That we should not lament when she hath done a
    bitter turn,
But thank her in that she
Hath held her hand from greater injury.

Tać jest władza Fortuny, mój najmilszy synie,
Że nie tak uskarzać się, kiedy nam co ginie,
Jako dziękować trzeba, że wżdam co zostało . . .
                                    (129–131)

Eminently rational advice, of the sort Seneca frequently gave, now follows: "Gaze at the happiness thou dost retain; / What is not loss, that must be rated gain." One of the poet's purposes in writing and printing the laments is revealed: "To other men in sorrow thou hast shown / The comfort left them . . . Time is the cure / For all." Kochanowski paraphrases Seneca (*Ad Marciam* iv) in his mother's last lines: "Bear man's portion like a man, my son; / The Lord of grief and comfort is but one," which refer to the statement "Nor will I urge upon you harsher precepts so as to bid you to endure our human lot in a manner superior to humanity."

The poet wakes: and "knows not if to deem / This truth itself, or but a fleeting dream."

X *Mythology*

The intermingling of elements in the cycle drawn from Christianity of a humanistic kind (not from any particular creed) and the pagan myths of Classical antiquity is a characteristic feature of Kochanowski's outlook. Classical symbols abound in the earlier part of the cycle: the Islands of the Blest, the "hidden chambers of the dead," the Philomela myth (X), and "those gates through which so long ago / Orpheus descended to the realms below" (XIV). The Orpheus myth was, of course, a harbinger of Christianity, and Kochanowski's use of it is an example of the way in which he and other Renaissance writers tried to connect the gods and goddesses of ancient Olympus to the Christian world.[12] Their attempts, often successful, are reflected in the findings of twentieth-century students of mythology, who have discovered that mythological themes repeat themselves in Christianity—rebirth, the archetypes (the Virgin Mary as "anima," or "the dark night of the soul").[13]

At this point, we may appropriately turn back to the quotation from the *Odyssey* which Kochanowski uses as an epigraph to the cycle (page 116). Ray J. Parrott, Jr. has pointed out that, in addition to being the first mythological allusion in the laments, the introductory epigraph "relates directly to the first point of reference to be considered ... and expresses the theme of the transitory quality of human fortune."[14] The following passage precedes the epigraph in the original text:

Of all creatures that breathe and walk on earth, there is nothing more helpless than a man is, of all the earth fosters; for he thinks that he will never suffer misfortune in future days, while the gods grant him courage and his knees have spring in them. But when the blessed gods bring sad days upon him, he must against his will suffer them with enduring spirits.

The allusion to Jupiter also evokes a wider context and points to the larger theme of the cycle: the conflict between Christian humanism and pagan wisdom. The pagan authors referred to in Lament I enable Kochanowski to take his place in the great literary traditions of poetry concerned with grief, lamentation, and death.

Other archetypal figures include Niobe (IV), and Proserpine, the wife of Pluto, who reigned as queen of death. Kochanowski points to her "sternness" and calls her "evil" (II, V). Charon appears, ferrying the souls of the dead "over the gloomy river" of Lethe (Styx), giving them "the water of oblivion" to drink (X).

But the references to pagan mythology are less frequent after Lament XV. The remaining four draw primarily on Christian and Biblical associations. Lament XVI, indeed, marks a turning point in the conflict here recorded by Kochanowski between pagan rationalism and Christian faith. The tone of Laments XVII and XVIII is reminiscent of certain of the Psalms. The writings of pagan philosophers (Lucretius, Cicero, Seneca) provided no answer to his desperate questionings. In the last resort, Christian humanism was to symbolize for him the only way to attain peace of mind.

XI   *The* Laments *in Polish Poetry*

Kochanowski's cycle established a long-standing tradition in Polish poetry, extending through the Baroque of the seventeenth century and Romanticism to our own time. A year after the death of the poet in 1584, Sebastian Klonowic (author of the allegorical poem *The Boatman*) composed a cycle of thirteen laments mourning Kochanowski's death, admitting that the only Polish poet of sufficient genius to write poetry worthy of Kochanowski's memory was Kochanowski himself.

Of course, poets of different epochs valued and admired aspects of Kochanowski's laments according to their own lights. Seventeenth-century poets like Samuel Twardowski, Wespasjan Kochowski, and Wacław Potocki were not much interested in Kochanowski's humanistic speculations; but the theme of Death continue to preoccupy them.[15] In addition, they admired the cyclic structure of Kochanowski's laments, since most Baroque writers were conscious of form in art, as witness the "shaped poems" (literally shaped like an object, circle, triangle, and the like). They replaced Kochanowski's philosophical meditations with banalities and panegyrics, emphasizing the virtues of the dead person and describing his death and funeral pomp.

As was the case with all of Kochanowski's popular works, so too later poets drew heavily on the vocabulary and poetic diction of the laments. Thus we find borrowings, quotations, reminiscences in much of the poetry of grief for the next two hundred years. Nor was the cult of Kochanowski's laments restricted to the major writers already mentioned; a large number of amateur versifiers flourished in Poland, often composing funeral poetry on the occasion of the death of a relative or friend. The laments were also plundered by theoreticians of poetics, composing the treatises for use in schools and colleges which the amateur poets took as their models. Consequently, the "literary heritage" of Kochanowski's laments tended to appear in the second-rate (or even third-rate) writers.

Polish Baroque declined sadly after the 1690's, when the most interesting poets died, leaving the style in decay for the next fifty years. But the Age of Enlightenment under King Stanisław August (Poniatowski) began in 1764, and among-works indebted to Kochanowski's laments were the *Laments of Orpheus upon Eurydice* (Żale Orfeusza and Eurydyką, 1783) by Franciszek Kniaźnin. The twenty-two laments were composed on the occasion of the death of a friend's wife. The contemporary critic and theoretician Franciszek Dmochowski esteemed the work highly for its "delicacy of writing, sensitivity of expression," which "place it alongside Kochanowski's laments." Kniaźnin was an admirer of Kochanowski, and translated the entire cycle of laments into Latin (Warsaw, 1781). However, his laments are in the idyllic manner, and their tone is (naturally enough) different from that of the original cycle. To be sure, the idyll had been used by Polish poets for lamenting deaths, but this was a development of a time later than Kochanowski's.

Echoes of the laments are to be heard in other kinds of Old Polish poetry. In a collection of spiritual songs, hymns, and psalms (Cantional pieśni duchownych, hymnów i psalmów...) published by the Czech Brethren in Toruń (1611), there is an anonymous paraphrase of Kochanowski's Lament XVII, with a changed ending. This version became a religious song or hymn and was reprinted, like the celebrated "Song" of 1564, in popular hymnbooks throughout the seventeenth and eighteenth centuries.[16]

Kochanowski's vocabulary and phraseology penetrated also into patriotic poetry, especially into the many elegies and complaints of the Polish Republic, composed on the occasion of various political misfortunes. Many writers also refer to Kochanowski's earlier, political poetry (*The Satyr*), with its often pessimistic warnings of various disasters liable to occur to Poland if her citizens did not mend their ways.

Romantic poets who developed the theme of death included Juliusz Słowacki (1809–1849). In his "eastern tale" in verse, *Father of the Plague-stricken* (Ojciec zadżumionych), he describes the grief of a father whose children have been carried off by plague: "O grief is known to none, / Like unto that which is today closed into my heart!"

Poets of our own time have looked back to Kochanowski's laments for consolation in similar circumstances. Bolesław Leśmian (died 1937), in his "Ursula Kochanowska," alludes to Lament VIII, where Kochanowski had predicted the child's future virtues, had she lived. Similarly, Władysław Broniewski (died 1962) composed a cycle entitled *Anka* following the death of a daughter, mourning the "emptiness" by which he was surrounded after her departure. Again, the allusion is to Lament VIII.

XII Wider Echoes

Professor Janusz Pelc, the foremost Kochanowski scholar of our time, holds that the *Laments* constitute the poet's finest work, and refers to the words of Adam Mickiewicz who, lecturing in Paris at the College de France in 1841, claimed that "We find nothing similar to the Laments in the literature of any country." The number of separate editions printed amounts to over fifty, and this figure does not take into account the number of times that the *Laments* have been included in collected or selected works of the poet. The popular "National Library" (Biblioteka Narodowa) series has published thirteen editions between 1919 and the present. Successive generations of Poles continue to admire and love the cycle.

Outside Poland, and in translation, the *Laments* were probably not known until the eighteenth century, when lines were quoted in handbooks of poetics in Ruthenian colleges and the Kiev Academy. Lament X appeared in German in a magazine (Tubingen, 1822), with two more in 1826. Sir John Bowring's anthology *Specimens of the Polish Poets* (London, 1827) contains five laments, as well as other of Kochanowski's poems. The volume was reprinted in 1832, and all Bowring's Kochanowski translations appeared in Paul Sobolewski's *Poets and Poetry of Poland* (Chicago, 1881). These again were reprinted in 1929, and in *The Polish Review* in 1943.

Six laments in Russian translation appeared in St. Petersburg in 1842. Mickiewicz translated parts of the cycle into French prose for his College de France lectures. More prose versions in French were published in Paris (1876, 1881), along with verse translations of the entire cycle (1884), although in obscure journals or newspapers. Other German translations continued to appear at intervals during the nineteenth century.

Six laments in Czech were published in 1878, while a free

translation based on Mickiewicz's French version of Lament XIX appeared in Italian (1865), followed by versions in Italian prose (1886).

The twentieth century brings a considerable increase in the number of translations: Czech (1903, 1928), the entire cycle in Italian blank verse (1926), Russian (1916, 1947, 1960), French (1919), German (1929). English versions include Dorothea Prall's complete version (1920, 1928); Professor Watson Kirkconnell's version of Lament I (1936), which was reprinted in 1943 and 1944; and two laments translated by Jerzy Peterkiewicz and Burns Singer, which appeared in the anthology *Five Centuries of Polish Poetry* (London, 1960; new edition, 1972).

Translations into lesser-known languages include the Romanian version (1941), Swedish (1918, partial), Hebrew (1928), and Slovak (1970).

CHAPTER 9

Conclusion

K OCHANOWSKI'S poetry looks "deceptively simple." But this is because he consistently followed classical poetics, which required a poet to conceal the "laboratory" aspect of his work and give it the impression of being apparently effortless and smooth. All poets of the sixteenth century considered themselves imitators of a world already created; they themselves were not "creative artists" in the way that poets have been since the appearance of Romanticism.

Undoubtedly, Kochanowski's greatest achievement was his transformation of the Polish language as a medium for poetry. He established the thirteen-syllable line for poetry of the loftiest kind (in the *Psalms*), the eleven-syllable line for narrative poetry (*A Game of Chess*), also using nine- and ten-syllable lines on occasion. He experimented within these limits with the placing of caesurae (e.g., four syllables followed by the caesura and five syllables; and vice versa). His handling of the caesura was original and gave later poets a model: although the metrical pattern of a line is syllabic, a stress is heard on the penultimate syllable before the caesura and also on the penultimate syllable of a line:

Czego chcesz od nas, Panie, za twe hojne dary

He introduced the run-on line (enjambement) which contributes to the smoothness of verse:

Żałość moja długo w noc oczu mi nie dała
Zamknąć. . . . (Lament XIX)

In this instance, the effect is one of meditative grief, as befits the poet's state of mind. In other examples, the flow of expres-

136

sion continues through two, three, or more lines, maintaining the rhythm and linking the lines with rhymes, thus avoiding the monotonous break at the end of every line, characteristic of earlier verse (especially that of Mikołaj Rej). Significantly, his earlier work such as *A Game of Chess* offers few examples of run-on lines (though printed texts are still unreliable bibliographically).

Kochanowski's sensitive ear was evidently offended by monosyllabic (masculine) rhymes, and his deliberate avoidance of such barbarisms succeeded in banishing them from Polish poetry entirely, until the Romantics (Adam Mickiewicz, among others) rediscovered that they might nevertheless be used for certain poetic purposes in "low" genres such as ballads.

But these are technical innovations, inherited and transplanted into Polish from Italian and Latin poetry, and Kochanowski's importance as a poet does not depend merely on them.

I *Minor Writings*

Not everything in Kochanowski's poetry is poetically alive today. He wrote verses required of him by patrons. Dry didacticism and earnest moralizing occupy space in his collected Polish works, which amount to over seven hundred and fifty pages of small type. His Latin poetry occupies another two hundred and fifty pages. But no major poet who composed so copiously produced work that was always of the first class. Yet some of the minor works were in fact written at the same time as the major poetry; the *Laments* were being written when he composed two of the most pedestrian pieces, *Jezda do Moskwy* (The Journey to Muscovy) and *Epitalamium na wesele Radziwiłła* (Radziwill's Epithalamium), neither of which has been described in this study. Both are technically interesting, to be sure, but otherwise lifeless.

II *His Place in Literature*

Kochanowski developed little during his twenty years of writing poetry. His "Song" (quoted on page 48) was first printed in 1562, and tradition says he wrote it three years earlier. Nor was there any decline in his powers, with the *Dismissal of the Grecian Envoys* and the *Laments* in 1578 and 1580, respectively. He had preferred topics, expressed in short forms —songs and epigrams—on love and friendship, domesticity and the pleasures of country life. To be sure, there are contradictions to be found in his work; he was persistently concerned with various questions which he was never able to answer to his own satisfaction. He could never decide, for instance, whether God or Chance (Fortuna) rules the fate of man. But nobody else has been able to answer that, either.

During his lifetime, Kochanowski's poetry was known to his contemporaries not only in printed books, but in manuscript copies. It had therefore a considerably wider circulation than might at first be supposed. Mikołaj Rej in his *Zoo* (Zwierzyniec, 1562) compares Kochanowski's work to that of Tibullus, the reference presumably being to Kochanowski's Latin elegies, and more than one, since Rej's phrase is "as his many writings clearly show." Łukasz Górnicki's *Polish Courtier* (Dworzanin polski, 1566), already mentioned in this study, contains a reference that suggests Kochanowski began writing poetry in Polish as early as 1549. He also refers to the *Epigrams*, which proves that Kochanowski had composed a number of them before 1566. They must have circulated in manuscript, as the first edition was not printed until 1584 (posthumously). Other references in Old Polish literature have been collated by Professor Janusz Pelc.[1]

Immediately after the poet's death (1584), his collected works were reprinted in remarkable numbers; by 1639, they had been reprinted twelve times, with twelve editions of the *Epigrams* alone. Even more remarkable than these figures is the fact that the *Psalms* went into nineteen editions by 1641, not to mention some for which the dates have not yet been established, and may for one reason or another be falsified. There were two separate editions of the *Songs* (1586, 1589), one more of the *Laments* (1585), *A Game of Chess* (ca. 1585) and of earlier poems. His Latin poetry was reprinted less often.

Remarkable though these figures are for the seventeenth century in Poland, the editions themselves appear to have been small, perhaps five hundred copies on the average, sometimes as many as a thousand. Nor do the figures take into account, when estimating the circulation of Kochanowski's work, the frequency with which his more popular psalms, laments, and songs were included in collections of hymnbooks, both Catholic and Protestant. His authorship was sometimes not acknowledged, and the texts themselves were paraphrased or abbreviated.

III *Hymnbooks and Manuscripts*

After 1670, Protestant hymnbooks, often containing one or more of Kochanowski's poems, began appearing in Polish in Silesia. Their reprinting throughout the eighteenth century played a significant part in the preservation of the language, as the region was threatened by "Germanification." The same applies to the "Prussian hymnbooks" printed in Polish for the subjects of the Elector of Brandenburg and the King of Prussia, who lived in Mazovia and on the Baltic and used the Polish language.

From what we know of the poet's religious faith, it is not surprising that the Protestants should have adopted his poems for their own purposes. To be sure, they did not hesitate to alter poems when they saw fit to do so. Sometimes, they even claimed that Kochanowski had been a Protestant, though Catholics denied this. But the fact remains that Kochanowski nowhere refers to the Virgin Mary or the saints. Yet, to complicate matters, Kochanowski dedicated his *Psalms* to Piotr Myszkowski, a Catholic bishop.

Catholic hymnbooks of the eighteenth century contain a considerable number of Kochanowski's psalms, and also the song "What would you of us, O Lord" (Czego chcesz od nas, Panie). Many hymnbooks survive in manuscript copies also, indicating the importance attributed to them and the scarcity of printed books. Often, too, the psalms or songs were printed without the author's name, or simply with the initials J. K., which means that the works themselves had taken root in Polish culture, and were not revered for their authorship alone. Moreover, the manuscript copies often indicate, by textual variants, that the scribes relied on their not always reliable memories, rather than a printed text.

As might be expected, many of the copies are of smaller things, rather than entire works, though there exists in the library of the Ossolineum Institute, Wroclaw, a handwriten copy of the *Psalms* made to look like print. This curiosity probably dates from the mid-seventeenth century, being a characteristic example of the Baroque fondness for paradox (something which refutes the evidence of the senses by looking like what it is not).

When printers ceased producing new editions of Kochanowski's work, around 1650, the handwritten copies proliferated, usually in the form of single songs, laments, or epigrams, often in collections or anthologies containing the writings of others, and provided with elaborately drawn and ornamented title pages. Many of these collections were destroyed during World War II, with an irreparable loss to Polish literature. They were disregarded by most (though not all) Polish scholars until interest was renewed in the literature of the seventeenth century (Brückner, Porembowicz). Even those collections which survived have not yet been thoroughly explored, and there is a possibility that others may come to light in archives and elsewhere, containing more copies of Kochanowski's poetry and demonstrating, as do those which exist, a continued admiration for it.

IV *Translations in Old Polish*

Maciej Sarbiewski (1595–1640), the Polish poet who wrote in Latin and was celebrated all over Europe for his works (he was known as the "Christian Horace"), translated some of Kochanowski's songs into Latin. Others, Sarbiewski paraphrased and altered. Although he wrote in Latin, Sarbiewski modeled his verses on Kochanowski in both content and style, though the language was that of Horace.

But translations into Latin of Kochanowski's poems contributed less to the development of Polish poetry than translations of his Latin poems into Polish, which began appearing as early as 1609 and continued into the eighteenth century and our own day. Not all the Latin elegies and epigrams were translated, however.

Selected psalms were translated into Lithuanian as early as 1598, with parallel texts; a handful of epigrams, *The Muse*, and one song appeared in Czech in the same year, with a version of the "Song" by Jan Komensky. The latter was printed in a hymnbook published in Amsterdam (1659), and was printed again in 1696. The "Song" also appeared in German, the translation being made by the Silesian Michal Henrica; it was printed in Leszno in 1639, with later editions which included one in Berlin (1731). More of Kochanowski's works which were translated into German include several psalms, and the Silesian poet Martin Opitz praises them in his own translation of the *Psalms* (1637). The fame of Kochanowski's psalms in Muscovy, the Ukraine, and the territories that are now Romania and Hungary has been mentioned in chapter 6.

V *Posthumous Fame*

In the second book of *Songs*, Kochanowski predicted his own celebrity:

> Muscovy and the Tatars will know of me,
> And the English, inhabitants of a different world;
> The German and the bold Spaniard will recognize me,
> And those who drink the deep river Tiber.

> O mnie Moskwa i będą wiedzieć Tatarowie;
> I różnego miszkańcy świata Anglikowie;
> Mnie Niemiec i waleczny Hiszpan, mnie poznają,
> Którzy głęboki strumień Tybrowy pijają.

> (II, xxiv)

Elsewhere in his work we find other references by the poet to the widespread popularity of his poems in his own country In the epigraph of the first edition of the *Songs* (1586), Kochanowski declares that "I give my books to nobody, or rather to everyone," and indeed he was the first Polish poet whose work gained a wide circulation and became "the property of the entire nation." ("Nobody" in this quotation refers to his literary heirs, of whom—though he had imitators—there was nobody to take his place.) The numerous editions published in the present century continue to bear witness to this.

In the first instance, of course, Kochanowski's heritage was passed down to poets, no matter whether they were major or minor figures in the history of Polish literature. His writings formed a direct link for the "Sarmatian" poets who knew little or nothing of the poetry of Classical antiquity or of Petrarch and his school. Polish poetry owes its great debt to Horace and Anacreon—especially in the eighteenth century—and to Kochanowski as intermediary. He established the basic repertoire of genres and verse stanzas in Old Polish poetry—satire, the cyclic laments, epigrams (indeed, Kochanowski invented the Polish name for the last-named "fraszki"), songs, and lyrical poetry.

But his many admirers and imitators, though they borrowed much from Kochanowski, were unable to compete with him in the expression of thought. This is not to claim that he was a particularly profound or original thinker—as already pointed out, he was a poet, not a philosopher—but he was clearly an individual who reflected and pondered long on matters that concerned him, and was able to express these reflections in poetry. In his serious poems, there is a depth of felt experience which his successors failed to reach, just as they could not match the lyricism of his songs, or the vitality of his epigrams, or the orotund wealth of his psalms.

Professor Tadeusz Ulewicz summed up Kochanowski's main achievement when he stated that the poet's genius lay in his ability to elevate Polish poetry to the level of European poetry. Kochanowski was the first Slavic poet to demonstrate that the "Slavic word" possesses the same strength, musicality, and beauty as any other language.[2]

Notes and References

Chapter One

1. *The Cambridge History of Poland* (Cambridge, 1950), I, 348. See also Władysław Pociecha, "Z dziejów stosunków kulturalnych polsko-włoskich" [From the History of Polish-Italian cultural Relations] (Warsaw, 1947), pp. 179–208, and Henryk Barycz, *Spojrzenia w przeszłość polsko-włoska* [Glances into the Polish-Italian Past] (Wrocław, 1965), pp. 205–43.

2. Pawel Jasienica, *Polska Jagiellonów* [Poland of the Jagiellons] (Warsaw, 1963), p. 387.

3. David Welsh, "Tasso in Eastern Europe," *Italica* XLVIII (3) (1971), 345–52.

4. Ignacy Chrzanowski, "Dlaczego Rej jest ojcem literatury polskiej" [Why Rej is Father of Polish Literature], *O literaturze polskiej* [On Polish Literature] (Warsaw, 1971), pp. 55–64. Originally published in 1905.

5. Janusz Pelc, *"Renesans w literaturze polskiej"* [The Renaissance in Polish Poetry] in Janusz Pelc, ed., *Problemy literatury staropolskiej, seria I [Problem of Old Polish Literature, First series]* (Wrocław, 1972), pp. 100–101.

6. Sebastjan Klonowicz, *The Boatman*, trans., M. M. Coleman (Cambridge Springs, Pa., 1958).

7. Stanisław Cynarski, *Reception of the Copernican Theory in Poland in the Seventeenth and Eighteenth Centuries* (Cracow, 1973), *passim.*

8. Antonina Jelicz, ed., *Antologia poezji polsko-łacińskiej* [Anthology of Polish-Latin Poetry] (Warsaw, 1956), covers the period from 1470 to 1543. See also Leon Witkowski, *Poeci nowołacińscy Torunia* [Neo-Latin Poets of Torun] (Torun, 1958), *passim.* Witkowski also describes the Neo-Latin poets of Danzig, Elbląg and Chełmno from 1359 to 1753.

9. F. R. Leavis, "Milton's Verse," *Scrutiny* II (1933), 130–31.

10. Frederic Raby, *The History of Christian Latin Poetry* (Oxford, 1953) remains the standard work in this field.

11. *Ibid.*, pp. 5–24.

12. *Ibid.*, pp. 50 ff.

13. Mieczysław Brahmer, *Petrarkizm w polskiej* [Petrarchism in Polish Poetry] (Cracow, 1927).

14. Tadeusz Ulewicz, "Na śladach Lidii padewskiej" [On the Traces of Lidia of Padua] in *Munera litteraria: księga ku czci profesora Romana Pollaka* [Munera littereria: Volume in Honor of Professor Roman Pollak] (Poznań, 1962), pp. 291–304.

15. Wiktor Weintraub, "Hellenizm Kochanowskiego a jego poetyka" [Kochanowski's Hellenism and his Poetics], *Pamiętnik literacki* [Literary Memoir], LVIII, no. 1 (1967), 1–25.

16. Translations include those by Andrew Sinclair, *Selections from the Greek Anthology* (London, 1967) and Peter Gay, *The Greek Anthology; a Selection* (London, 1973).

17. See F. O. Matthiessen, *Translation, an Elizabethan Art* (Cambridge, Mass., 1931) for details.

18. Described at greater length by David Welsh, "Il cortegiano polacco, 1564," *Italica* XL (1963), 22–27.

19. Tadeusz Ulewicz, "Epitaphium Cretcovii, czyli najstarszy dziś wiersz drukowany Jana Kochanowskiego" [Epitaph to Cretcovius, or the Oldest Printed Verse of Jan Kochanowski Known Today], in *Księga pamiątkowa ku czci Stanisława Pigonia* [Memorial Volume in Honor of Stanisław Pigoń] (Cracow, 1961), pp. 161–68.

20. William Lawton, *The Soul of the Anthology* (New Haven, 1923), p. 174.

Chapter Two

1. Stefan Świerczewski, "Kraszewski o języku Kochanowskiego, Sępa i Naruszewicza," *Poradnik językowy*, no. 3 (1956), 101–106, also discusses this topic.

2. Mieczysław Brahmer, *op. cit.*

3. See Stanisław Pigoń ed., *W kręgu "Gofreda" i "Orlanda"* [In the Circle of "Gofredo" and "Orlando"] (Wrocław, 1970), *passim*.

4. Janusz Tomiak, "The University of Cracow in its Period of Greatness," *Polish Review* XVI, no. 3 (1971), 94.

5. Stefania Skwarczyńska, "*Treny* a 'Sur la mort de Marie,'" [*The Laments* and "On the Death of Marie"] in *Kultura i literatura dawnej Polski* [The Culture and Literature of Old Poland] (Warsaw, 1968), pp. 101–39, being a recent example of such attempts.

Chapter Three

1. Jadwiga Rydel, *Jan Kochanowski* (Warsaw, 1967), p. 74.

2. Ihor Szewczenko, "Rozważania nad *Szachami* Jana Kochanow-

skiego" [Reflections on Kochanowski's *Game of Chess*], *Pamiętnik literacki* [Literary Memoir] LXVIII, no. 2 (1967), 341–61.

3. David Welsh, *Ignacy Krasicki* (New York, 1969), pp. 82–89 discusses this topic in more detail.

4. David Welsh, *Adam Mickiewicz* (New York, 1966), p. 115 discusses this topic in more detail.

5. Richard Bernheimer, *Wild Men in the Middle Ages* (Harvard, 1952), pp. 2–3, 113–14.

6. Claude Backvis, "Autour du *Satyre* de Jan Kochanowski," *Zagadnienia rodzajów literackich* [Problems of Literary Genres] I (1958), 17–44. See also Juliusz Nowak-Długoszewski, *Poemat satyryczny w literaturze polskiej w XVI–XVII ww* [The Satirical Poem in Sixteenth- and Seventeenth-Century Polish Literature] (Warsaw, 1962), pp. 9–20; Janusz Pelc, "Potomstwo *Satyra* Jana Kochanowskiego w poezji polskiej" [Descendants of Kochanowski's *Satyr* in Polish Poetry], *Pamiętnik literacki* [Literary Memoir] LIV, no. 4, (1963), 267–311, and the same author's "Oświeceniowa polemika ze staropolskim *Satyrem*" [An Age of Enlightenment Polemic with the Old Polish *Satyr*] in *Miscellanea z doby Oświecenia* [Miscellany from the Age of Enlightenment] (Warsaw, 1965), II, 5–16.

7. David Welsh, "Sienkiewicz's *Trilogy*: a Study in Novelistic Techniques," *Antemurale* XV (1971), 249–52.

8. Wacław Walecki, "Motyw Zuzanny i starców w literaturze polskiej" [The Motif of Susannah and the Elders in Polish Literature], *Rocznik Komisji historycznoliterackiej Polskiej Akademii Nauk* [Annual of the Literary History Commission of the Polish Academy of Sciences] 10 (1972), 27–48.

9. Wacław Borowy, *Studia i Rozprawy* [Studies and Essays] (Wrocław, 1952), I, 13.

10. Tadeusz Ulewicz, *Oddziaływanie europejskie Jana Kochanowskiego* [Kochanowski's European Influence], (Cracow, 1970), pp. 20–21.

Chapter Four

1. Wiktor Weintraub, quoted by Jadwiga Rydel, *op. cit.*, p. 204.

2. Leopold Sabourin, *The Psalms, Their Origins and Meaning* (New York, 1969), pp. 2–3.

3. C. S. Lewis, *Reflections on the Psalms* (London, 1958), *passim*.

4. Zofia Szmydtowa, *Poeci i poetyka* [Poets and Poetics] (Warsaw, 1965), pp. 69–85.

5. John Buxton, *Sir Philip Sidney and the English Renaissance*

(London, 1954), pp. 73, 152. See also Coburn Freen, "The Style of Sidney's *Psalms*," *Language and Style* II (1969), 64.

6. Jan Kasprzak, "A Riddle of History: Queen Elizabeth I and the Albertus Łaski Affair," *Polish Review* XIV, nos. 1 and 2 (1969), 53–67, 63–88.

7. Wiktor Weintraub, "Kochanowski's Renaissance Manifesto," *Slavonic and East European Review* XXX, no. 75 (1951), 422 ff., on Kochanowski's use of negative epithets generally. See also Stanisław Rospond, *Język i artyzm językowy Jana Kochanowskiego* [Language and Linguistic Artistry of Kochanowski] (Wrocław, 1960), pp. 201–206, listing the frequency of such epithets in four of Kochanowski's Polish works.

8. Grahame Castor, *Pléiade Poetics: a Study in Sixteenth Century Thought and Terminology* (Cambridge, 1964), p. 100.

9. Stanisław Rospond, *op. cit.*, *passim*.

10. X. P. Kwoczyński, *Psałterz Fr. Karpińskiego i jego stosunek do Psałterza Kochanowskiego* [Karpiński's *Psalter* and Its Relation to Kochanowski's *Psalms*] (Lublin, 1907).

11. Wacław Borowy, *O poezji polskiej w w. XVIII* [On Polish Poetry in the Eighteenth Century] (Cracow, 1948), *passim*.

12. I. Z. Serman, "*Psaltyr rifmotvornaja* Simeona Polotskogo" [Simeon Polotskii's *Rhymed Psalter*], *Trudy otdela drevnerusskoi literatury AN SSSR* [Publications of the Old Russian Literary Section of the Academy of Sciences of the USSR], XVIII (1962), 214–32.

13. Tadeusz Ulewicz, *Oddziaływanie europejskie . . . op. cit.*, pp. 6–19.

Chapter Five

1. Julian Krzyżanowski, *Romans polski* [The Polish Romance] (Warsaw, 1962), pp. 37–42. Kochanowski's play was translated into English by G. R. Noyes in his *Poems of Jan Kochanowski* (Berkeley, 1928), pp. 81–113. This translation has been drawn on for quotations in this chapter.

2. G. R. Noyes, *op. cit.*, p. 6.

3. S. H. Butcher, *Aristotle's Theory of Poetry and Fine Art* (New York, 1951), pp. 41–42. First published in 1911.

4. David Welsh, *Russian Comedy 1765–1823* (The Hague, 1966), pp. 115–18.

5. Wiktor Weintraub, "Teatr Seneki i struktura *Odprawy posłów greckich*" [Senecan Drama and the Structure of *The Dismissal of the Grecian Envoys*] in *Studia o literaturze dawnej Polski* [Studies in the Literature of Old Poland] (Warsaw, 1968), p. 96. J. Kultaniakowa,

Odprawa posłów greckich wobec tragedji renesansowej [*Dismissal of the Grecian Envoys* compared to Renaissance Tragedy] (Poznań, 1963) was not available to the present writer.

6. Czesław Miłosz, *History of Polish Literature* (New York, 1969), p. 74.

7. *Ibid.*, p. 75.

8. *Ibid.*, p. 73.

Chapter Six

1. For an account of the emblem book in Poland, see David Welsh, "Zbigniew Morsztyn and the Emblem Tradition," *Symposium* XIX, no. 1 (1965), 80–84.

2. Janusz Pelc, "Chronologia *Fraszek*" [Chronology of the *Fraszki*] in his introduction to Jan Kochanowski, *Fraszki* (Wrocław, 1957), pp. lxiv–lxvi.

3. Czesław Miłosz, *op. cit.*, p. 64.

4. W. H. Auden, *Forwords and Afterwords* (New York, 1973), pp. 88–108.

5. J. Bailbé, "Le thcme de la vieille femme dans le poésie satirique du 16-ième siècle," *Bibliotheque de l'Humanisme* XXVI (1964), 98–119. See also Władysław Floryan, *Forma poetycka 'Pieśni' Jana Kochanowskiego* [Poetic Form of Kochanowski's 'Songs'] (Wrocław, 1948), p. 45.

6. For an account of this individual, see Tomasz Fijałkowski, *Piotr Rojzjusz w opiniach współczesnych i potomnych* [Piotr Rojzjusz in Contemporary and Later Opinions] (Łódź, 1972).

7. Howard Patch, *The Goddess Fortuna in Medieval Literature* (New York, 1967), provides a thorough survey of the topic.

8. Anna Motto, *Seneca Sourcebook* (Amsterdam, 1970), *passim*.

Chapter Seven

1. See, for instance, Zofia Głombiowska, "Inspiracje propercjańskie w elegiach Jana Kochanowskiego" [Propertian Inspirations in Jan Kochanowski's *Elegies*], *Pamiętnik literacki* [Literary Memoir] LXIII, no. 3 (1972), 5–28, and Jan Błoński, *Mikołaj Sęp-Szarzyński a początki polskiego baroku* [Sęp-Szarzyński and the Beginnings of Polish Baroque] (Cracow, 1967), p. 230.

2. Władysław Floryan, *op. cit.*, p. 64.

3. Wacław Borowy, *Studia i rozprawy* [Studies and Essays] (Wrocław, 1952), I, 22.

4. Steele Commager, *The Odes of Horace* (New Haven, 1962), pp. 143–44.

5. For examples, see Arthur T. Hatto, ed., *Eros: an Inquiry into the Theme of Lovers' Meetings at Dawn* (London, 1965), *passim*.

6. Howard Patch, *op. cit.*, pp. 26–27.

7. M. Putnam, *Virgil's Pastoral Art* (New Jersey, 1970), pp. 3, 9–14.

8. Edward W. Taylor, *Nature and Art in Renaissance Literature* (New York, 1964), pp. 5–6.

9. Tadeusz Ulewicz, *Świadomość słowiańska Jana Kochanowskiego* [Jan Kochanowski's Slavonic Consciousness] (Cracow, 1948), pp. 69 ff. This section draws largely on Professor Ulewicz's work.

10. G. Lowall, *Theocritus' Coan Pastorals* (Washington, 1957), p. 5. See also Zofia Szmydtowa, "Owidiuszowe nuty w *Sobótce* Kochanowskiego" [Ovidian Notes in Kochanowski's *St. John's Eve*] in *Munera litteraria, op. cit.*, pp. 279–84.

11. Janusz Pelc, "Rękopiśmienna wersja *Sobótki* Jana Kochanowskiego" [A Manuscript Version of Jan Kochanowski's *St. John's Eve*], *Miscellanea staropolskie* [Old Polish Miscellany] (Wrocław, 1969), III, 9–34. Facsimiles included.

Chapter Eight

1. Jerzy Pietrkiewicz, "The Mediaeval Dream Formula in Kochanowski's *Laments*," *Slavonic and East European Review* XXXI, no. 77 (1953), 388–91. The *Laments* in English translation were published in G. R. Noyes *et al.*, *Poems of Jan Kochanowski* (*op. cit.*), pp. 19–52.

2. Teresa Kruszewska, "Funeralna poezja Jana Kochanowskiego na tle poezji renesansowej" [Kochanowski's Funeral Poetry against the Background of Renaissance Poetics], *Prace literackie* [Literary Works] I (1956), 173–87.

3. Mary Evaristus, *The Consolations of Death in Ancient Greek Literature* (Washington, n.d.), *passim*. See also Velma Richmond, *Laments for the Dead in Medieval Narrative Poetry* (Pittsburgh, 1966), pp. 13–37.

4. T. S. Eliot, "Shakespeare and the Stoicism of Seneca," quoted by John Mersereau Jr., in "Jan Kochanowski's *Laments*: a Definition of the Emotion of Grief," *Studies in Russian and Polish Literature in Honor of Wacław Lednicki* (The Hague, 1962), p. 38.

5. Roman Pollak, "Na marginesie drugiego z *Trenów* Jana Kochanowskiego" [In the Margin of the Second of Kochanowski's Laments], *Pamiętnik literacki* [Literary Memoir] XXVII, no. 2, 302–303.

6. David Welsh, *Ignacy Krasicki* (New York, 1969), p. 28.

7. Wiktor Weintraub, "Fraszka in a Tragic Key," *Janua linguarum* XXXIII (1967), 2219–30.

8. David Welsh, *op. cit.*, p. 84.

9. Ray J. Parrott, Jr., "Mythological Allusions in Kochanowski's *Laments*," *Polish Review* XIV, no. 1 (1969), 3–19.

10. David Daiches, "On Translating the Hebrew Bible," in his *Literary Essays* (Chicago, 1966), pp. 193–97.

11. Jerzy Pietrkiewicz, *op. cit.*, *passim*.

12. Mieczysław Hartleb, *Nagróbka Urzulki* [Ursula's Tomb] (Cracow, 1927), pp. 12–14.

13. For an account of the archetypes, see Carl G. Jung, ed., *Man and His Symbols* (New York, 1970), pp. 123 ff.

14. Ray J. Parrott, Jr., *op. cit.*, p. 4.

15. Janusz Pelc, *"Treny" Jana Kochanowskiego* [Jan Kochanowski's "Laments"] (Warsaw, 1972), pp. 127–47.

16. Janusz Pelc, *Jan Kochanowski w tradycjach literatury polskiej* [Jan Kochanowski in the Traditions of Polish Literature] (Warsaw, 1965), pp. 82 ff. This chapter draws largely on Professor Pelc's work.

Conclusion

1. Janusz Pelc, *Jan Kochanowski w tradycjach . . . op. cit.*, *passim*.

2. Tadeusz Ulewicz, *Świadomość słowiańska . . .* [Slavic Consciousness . . .] *op cit.*, p. 100.

Selected Bibliography

BIBLIOGRAPHIES IN POLISH

HERNAS, CZESŁAW. "Badania naukowe literatury staropolskiej w powojennym dwudziestopięćoleciu" [Scholarly Research in Old Polish Literature for the Past Twenty-five years]. *Prace literackie* [Literary Works] XIV (1972), pp. 5–22. A general survey concentrating on authors, genres and specific problems of various natures (e.g., linguistic).

INSTYTUT BADAŃ LITERACKICH. *Polska bibliografia literacka* [Polish literary bibliography]. Warsaw: Polska Akademia Nauk, in progress. Currently being published with a three-year delay, e.g., the volume for 1969 was published in 1972. Includes some items in languages other than Polish.

PIEKARSKI, KAZIMIERZ. *Bibliografia dzieł Jana Kochanowskiego: wiek XVI–XVII* [Bibliography of the Works of Jan Kochanowski: XVI and XVII Centuries]. Cracow: Polska Akademia Umiejętności, 1934. Full bibliographical descriptions of all known editions of the poet's works for the period.

POLLAK, ROMAN ET AL. *Bibliografia literatury polskiej "Nowy Korbut"* 2. *Piśmiennictwo staropolskie* [Bibliography of Polish Literature "New Korbut" 2. Old Polish Literature]. Warsaw: Państwowy Instytut Wydawniczy, 1964. The Polish national bibliography. Works of all known authors are classified, then arranged chronologically with references to critical and other studies. No annotations, and much fugitive material, e.g., in newspapers and provincial magazines.

STAROWOLSKI, SZYMON. *Setnik pisarzów polskich* [Century of Polish Writers]. Cracow: Wydawnictwo Literackie, 1970. First printed in Latin (Frankfurt, 1625), this edition has been edited and translated into Polish by Jerzy Starnawski. Starowolski's information is not always reliable, but his book contains the first bio-bibliography of Kochanowski.

BIBLIOGRAPHY IN ENGLISH

COLEMAN, MARION M. *Polish Literature in English Translation.* Cheshire, Conn.: Cherry Hill Books, 1963. Comprehensive, but lacks annotations, and poems in obscure journals are listed. Lists Kochanowski's works on pp. 42–46.

PRIMARY SOURCES

KOCHANOWSKI, JAN. *Dzieła polskie* [Polish Works] edited with an introduction by Julian Krzyżanowski. Warsaw: Państwowy Instytut Wydawniczy, 1960. Notes, indexes and a list of unfamiliar words are included. The editor contributes a note on bibliographical problems (pp. 955–62). For Kochanowski's Latin poetry see Jan Kochanowski, *Dzieła wszystkie. Wydanie kompletne* [Complete Works. Complete Edition]. Four volumes. Warsaw: Orgelbrand, 1884–1897. The Latin texts are contained in volume 3, with Polish versions by T. Krasnosielski. A new edition of the complete works under the auspices of the Polish Academy of Sciences Institute of Literary Research has been announced for 1972–1982.

ENGLISH TRANSLATION

NOYES, GEORGE R. ET AL. *Poems of Jan Kochanowski*. Berkeley: University of California, 1928. Long out of print, the volume contains the complete *Laments* and *Dismissal of the Grecian Envoys* skillfully rendered into English verse. The translations have been used, sometimes with slight variations, in the present study.

SECONDARY SOURCES IN POLISH

BARYCZ, HENRYK. *Spojrzenia w przeszłość polska-włoską* [Glances into the Polish-Italian Past]. Wrocław: Ossolineum, 1965. Professor Barycz draws upon his immense erudition in this collection of essays on Polish-Italian relations over the centuries.

BŁOŃSKI, JAN. *Mikołaj Sęp-Szarzyński a początki polskiego baroku* [M. Sęp-Szarzyński and the Origins of Polish Baroque]. Cracow: Wydawnictwo literackie, 1967. Discusses the literary relations between Sęp-Szarzyński and Kochanowski in a wide context.

BOROWY, WACŁAW. *O poezji polskiej w wieku XVIII* [On Polish Poetry of the XVIIIth Century]. Cracow: Polska Akademia Umiejętności, 1948. The first extensive study of the poetry and writers of the Polish Age of Enlightenment.

——————. *Studia i rozprawy* [Studies and Essays], two volumes. Wrocław: Ossolineum, 1952. Several essays on aspects of Kochinowski's life and work appear in vol. I.

BRAHMER, MIECZYSŁAW. *Petrarkizm w poezji polskiej XVI w.* [Petrarchism in Sixteenth Century Polish Poetry]. Cracow: Kasa im. Mianowskiego, 1927. One of Professor Brahmer's earliest publications, this work remains the most comprehensive study of its kind in Polish comparative studies.

FLORYAN, WŁADYSŁAW. *Forma poetycka "Pieśni" Jana Kochanowskiego* [Poetical Form of Kochanowski's "Songs"]. Wrocław: Państwowy Instytut Wydawniczy, 1948. Originally a dissertation, the work concentrates on the *Songs* in relation to lyrical poetry of the Renaissance and the poetry of Horace.

GŁOMBIOWSKA, ZOFIA. "Inspiracje propercjańskie w elegiach Jana Kochanowskiego." [Propertian Inspirations in Kochanowski's elegies]. *Pamiętnik literacki* [Literary Memoir] LXIII, no. 3 (1972), 5–28. Of the three Latin poets (Tibullus, Gallus, and Propertius) whose elegies were models for those of Kochanowski, Głombiowska proposes that the last-named was the most influential.

HARTLEB, MIECZYSŁAW. *Nagrobka Urszulki* [Ursula's Tomb]. Cracow: Krakowska Spółka Wydawnicza, 1927. The unwarranted diminutives in Hartleb's title indicate his sentimental approach to Kochanowski's *Laments*. The work is no longer considered reliable in its speculations.

HERNAS, CZESŁAW. *Barok* [The Baroque]. Warsaw: Państwowe Wydawnictwo Naukowe, 1973. Although Kochanowski's poetry is not Baroque in any way, its importance in the seventeenth century is examined here.

JASIENICA, PAWEŁ. *Polska Jagiellonów* [Poland of the Jagiellons]. Warsaw: Państwowy Instytut Wydawniczy, 1963. A popular account by the late novelist and journalist.

JELICZ, ANTONINA, ed. *Antologia poezji polsko-łacińskiej* [Anthology of Polish-Latin Poetry]. Warsaw: Państwowy Instytut Wydawniczy, 1956. The editor provides an informative introduction to this neglected field.

KRUSZEWSKA, TERESA. "Funeralna poezja Jana Kochanowskiego na tle poetyki renansowej" [Kochanowski's Funeral Poetry against the Background of Renaissance Poetics] *Prace literackie* [Literary Works] I (1956), 173–87. The writer of this essay has since specialized in Baroque poetry; here, she covers a wide area very briefly.

KRZYŻANOWSKI, JULIAN. *Romans polski* [Polish Romance]. Warsaw: Państwowy Instytut Wydawniczy, 1962. A collection of essays dealing with various aspects of the genre in sixteenth-century Poland.

Nowak-Dłużewski, Juliusz. *Poemat satyrowy w literaturze polskiej w XVI–XVII wiekach* [The Satirical Poem in Polish Literature of the XVIth and XVIIth Centuries]. Warsaw: Uniwersytet Warszawski, 1962. Special reference to Kochanowski's satirical poems on pp. 9–20.

Pelc, Janusz. "Chronologia *Fraszek*" [Chronology of the *Fraszki*]. In Introduction to Jan Kochanowski, *Fraszki*, pp. lxiv–lxvi. Wrocław: Ossolineum, 1957. A summing-up of the complex problem.

––––––. *Jan Kochanowski w tradycjach literatury polskiej* [Kochanowski in the Traditions of Polish Literature]. Warsaw: Państwowy Instytut Wydawniczy, 1965. A far-reaching study by the foremost Kochanowski scholar of the present day.

––––––. "Oświeceniowa polemika ze staropolskim *Satyrem*" [An Age of Enlightenment Polemic with the Old Polish Satyr]. In *Miscellanea z doby Oświecenia* [Miscellany from the Age of Enlightenment] II, 5–16. Warsaw: Instytut Badań Literackich, 1965. Though only a brief contribution to the volume, Professor Pelc draws attention to an interesting episode in Polish literary history.

––––––. "Rękopiśmienna wersja *Sobótki* Jana Kochanowskiego" [A Manuscript Version of Kochanowski's *St. John's Eve*]. In *Miscellanea staropolskie* [Old Polish Miscellany] III, 9–34. Wrocław: Ossolineum, 1969. A description of a manuscript version of the work, probably dating from the mid-seventeenth century, now preserved in the Czartoryski library, Cracow. The description is accompanied by a facsimile, somewhat reduced, of the original.

Pelc, Janusz, ed. *Problemy literatury staropolskiej* [Problems of Old Polish Literature]. First Series. Wrocław: Ossolineum, 1972. Professor Pelc contributes an extended essay on "Renesans w literatury polskiej; początki i rozwój" [The Renaissance in Polish Literature: Origins and Development], pp. 28–104, in which he discusses the place of Kochanowski in his era. He also contributes another essay "Sarmatyzm a Barok" [Sarmatism and Baroque], pp. 105–53.

––––––. "*Treny*" *Jana Kochanowskiego* [Kochanowski's *Laments*]. 2nd edition. Warsaw: Czytelnik, 1972. In addition to a close analysis of the text, Professor Pelc also provides critical remarks and judgments of the *Laments* by earlier scholars, as well as listing translations of the work into foreign languages.

Pigoń, Stanisław, ed. *W kręgu "Gofreda" i "Orlanda": Księga pamiątkowa Sesji naukowej Piotra Kochanowskiego* [In the

Circle of *Goffredo* and *Orlando*: Memorial Volume of the Scholarly Session on Piotr Kochanowski]. Wrocław: Ossolineum, 1970. A collection of papers on aspects of Tasso's *Goffredo* [Jerusalem Liberated] and Ariosto's *Orlando furioso*, both translated into Polish by Piotr Kochanowski (1566–1620). Papers by Professors Weintraub and Peterkiewicz are included.

ROSPOND, STANISŁAW. *Język i artyzm językowy Jana Kochanowskiego* [Language and Lingustic Artistry of Kochanowski]. Wrocław: Ossolineum, 1960. Essentially a linguistic study (as the title indicates), with word-counts and examination of Kochanowski's syntax, etc.

RYTEL, JADWIGA. *Jan Kochanowski*. Warsaw: Wiedza Powszechna, 1967. A popular biography based on thorough research.

SKWARCZYŃSKA, STEFANIA. "*Treny* Jana Kochanowskiego a cykl funeralny Ronsarda 'Sur la mort de Marie,' " [Kochanowski's *Laments* and Ronsard's Funeral Cycle "On the Death of Marie"]. In *Kultura i literatura dawnej Polski: Studia* [The Culture and Literature of Old Poland: Essays]. Warsaw: Państwowe Wydawnictwo Naukowe, 1968. A recent example of the unrewarding attempts to demonstrate literary relationships between similar works.

SŁOŃSKI, STANISŁAW. *O języku Jana Kochanowskiego* [On Kochanowski's Language]. Warsaw: Towarzystwo Naukowe Warszawskie, 1949. A pioneering work by the eminent linguist.

SOBACZKÓWNA, HELENA. *Jan Kochanowski jako tłumacz* [Kochanowski as Translator]. Poznań: Uniwersytet Poznański, 1934. Deals not only with the Psalms but with Kochanowski's little-known translations from Greek and Latin authors.

SZEWCZENKO, IHOR. "Rozważania nad *Szachami* Jana Kochanowskiego" [Reflections on Kochanowski's *Game of Chess*]. *Pamiętnik literacki* [Literary Memoir] LXVIII, no. 2 (1967), 341–61. A serious though entertaining account of Kochanowski's poem by the eminent scholar who (evidently) is also a player of chess himself.

SZMYDTOWA, ZOFIA. "Owidiuszowe nuty w *Sobótce* Kochanowskiego" [Ovidian Notes in Kochanowski's *St. John's Eve*]. In *Munera litteraria; Księga ku czci profesora Romana Pollaka* [Munera litteraria: Volume in Honor of Professor Roman Pollak]. Poznań: Państwowy Instytut Wydawniczy, 1962. Still another example of a convincing discovery of classical influences in Kochanowski's poetry; yet exercises of this learned sort assist little in approaching the work in question.

————. *Poeci i poetyka* [Poets and Poetics]. Warsaw: Państwowe

Wydawnictwo Naukowe, 1967. A collection of essays by the eminent scholar of poetry and poetics, including several on aspects of Kochanowski's art.

ULEWICZ, TADEUSZ. "Epitaphium Cretcovii, czyli najstarzy dziś wierz drukowany Jana Kochanowskiego" [The Epitaph to Cretcovius, or the Oldest Printed Verse of Kochanowski known Today]. In *Księga pamiątkowa ku czci Stanisława Pigonia* [Memorial Volume in Honor of Stanisław Pigoń]. Cracow: Wydawnictwo Literackie, 1961, pp. 161–68. An ingenious discovery by Professor Ulewicz, of archaeological and antiquarian interest.

————. "Na śladach Lidii padewskiej" [On Traces of Lidia of Padua]. In *Munera litteraria; księga ku czci profesora Romana Pollaka* (*op. cit.*) pp. 291–304. A scholarly though unprofitable attempt to "identify" the Lidia who appears in certain of Kochanowski's songs.

————. "Jan Kochanowski." In *Polski słownik biograficzny* [Polish Biographical Dictionary). Wrocław: Polska Akademia Nauk, Instytut Historii, vol. XIII (1967–68). The standard biographical dictionary, which has been appearing in installments since the 1930's.

————. *Oddziaływanie europejskie Jana Kochanowskiego* [European Influences of Kochanowski]. Cracow: Polska Akademia Nauk, 1970. Though brief (39 pp.) this essay covers a wide range of hitherto unknown facts about the appearance in various European literatures of Kochanowski's poems.

WEINTRAUB, WIKTOR. "Hellenizm Kochanowskiego a jego poetyka" [Kochanowski's Hellenism and his Poetics]. *Pamiętnik literacki* [Literary Memoir] LVIII, no. 1 (1967), 1–25. Professor Weintraub's interest in Kochanowski and his work extends over forty years. See next item.

————. *Styl Jana Kochanowskiego* [Kochanowski's Style]. Cracow: Kasa im. Mianowskiego, 1932. Still the finest study of its kind, and unlikely to be surpassed.

SECONDARY SOURCES IN OTHER LANGUAGES

REDDAWAY, W. F. ET AL. *The Cambridge History of Poland from the Origins to Sobieski (to 1696).* Cambridge: The University Press, 1950. Planned in 1936, this monumental work was eleven years in completion; it is likely to remain the standard history of the period for many years.

CYNARSKI, STANISŁAW. *Reception of the Copernican Theory in Poland in the Seventeenth and Eighteenth Centuries.* Cracow: Jagellonian University, 1973. Though short (63 pp.) this is a thorough survey of the topic and contains numerous illustrations. A version in Polish is also available.

MIŁOSZ, CZESŁAW. *A History of Polish Literature.* New York: Macmillan, 1969. The standard textbook in its field, this volume covers Polish literature from the origins to the present. It contains a selective bibliography, and extended quotations from texts appear in English and the original.

PARROTT, RAY J., JR. "Mythological Allusions in Kochanowski's *Laments." Polish Review* XIV, no. 1 (1969), 3–19. A thorough and scholarly examination of this important subject.

PETERKIEWICZ, JERZY. "The Mediaeval Dream Formula in Kochanowski's *Laments." Slavonic and East European Review* XXXI, no. 77 (1953), 388–401. An illuminating study of Kochanowski's use of a literary "formula" which he made his own.

SERMAN, I. Z. "*Psaltyr rifmotvornaja* Simeona Polotskogo" [Simeon Polotskii's *Rhymed Psalter*]. *Trudy otdela drevnerusskoi literatury AN SSSR* [Publications of the Section of Old Russian Literature of the Academy of Sciences of the USSR] XVIII (1962), 214–232. An account of Kochanowski's *Psalms* in the Russian version of Polotskii (seventeenth century).

Index

159